ISBN 9798563329737

WARNING!

This Book contains graphic images; some people will find disturbing. Open this Book and view its contents at your own risk!

<u>No person under 18 years of age should</u> view the contents of this Book!

THIS IS A PHOTO BOOK OF
The Bizarre, Dead, Atrocities, and WTF's?

The Strange World of Humans!

<u>DO NOT OPEN THIS BOOK UNLESS YOU ARE AT LEAST 18 YEARS OLD!</u>

By Dr. I.B. Gross

INTRODUCTION

It has been said; a picture is worth 1,000 words. Nothing could be more accurate. Few words, or none, are needed to understand and appreciate what you are about to view.

WARNING!

The images are graphic, and some people will find them upsetting, deplorable, unspeakable, disturbing, and disgusting. That is true.

Remember, people with medical disorders cannot be the object of laughter, cruel jokes, or ridicule. They are not responsible for their condition.

We must not forget the acts of violence and evil depicted in this Book, for they are the work of evil humans. You will know evil when you see it.

Most, if not all, of the people in this Book, now cry in silence from the grave. Hear them. Learn from them.

Remember, the only guarantee anyone has in life is the past. No one is guaranteed a tomorrow. Life can unexpectedly end in the blink of an eye. Spend time with the people you love. Tell them they hold a special place in your heart because their life or yours can end at any time.

Regarding war, the most critical aspect to remember is that presidents, kings, prime ministers, and dictators start wars; they never fight in wars. The soldier is the only person sacrificing their life during wars, not the politicians. Remember that fact when viewing the photographs of war injuries.

As a Doctor, I have witnessed the unspeakable cruelty inflicted by humans upon humans. Now you will see a few examples.

The photographs lack sharpness because they were taken over 100 years ago.

Dr. I. B. Gross

TABLE OF CONTENTS

NAZI WAR ATROCITIES...................................16

JAPANESE WAR ATROCITIES..........................33

AMERICAN CIVIL WAR INJURIES....................53

W.W. 1 INJURIES...61

THE BIZARRE, CRIME AND WTF?...................74

THE MOBSTERS...75

THE OUTLAWS...79

THE WTF'S?...89

THE MUMMIES..120

LYNCHING'S..130

SLAUGHTERING NATIVE AMERICANS..........134

VICTORIAN-ERA DEATH PHOTOGRAPHY.......140

HUMAN ODDITIES.......................................157

MEDIEVAL TORTURE...................................180

DEATH & SATAN IN MEDIEVAL TIMES..........195

THE WTF'S OF U.S. PATENTS.......................209

THIS IS YOUR LAST WARNING!

DO NOT GO BEYOND THIS PAGE IF VIEWING DEATH, HUMAN ODDITIES, TORTURE, AND EVIL UPSETS YOU!

THE NEXT SIX PAGES PROVIDE AN EXAMPLE OF WHAT IS CONTAINED IN THE BOOK. THESE ARE NOT THE MOST SHOCKING PICTURES.

IF YOU FIND THEM DISTURBING, CLOSE THE BOOK AND DO NOT REOPEN IT AGAIN!

Robert McGee
Scalped by Indians.

U.S. Navy blimp downed during a 1957 atomic bomb test.

Bulgarian dead 1900.

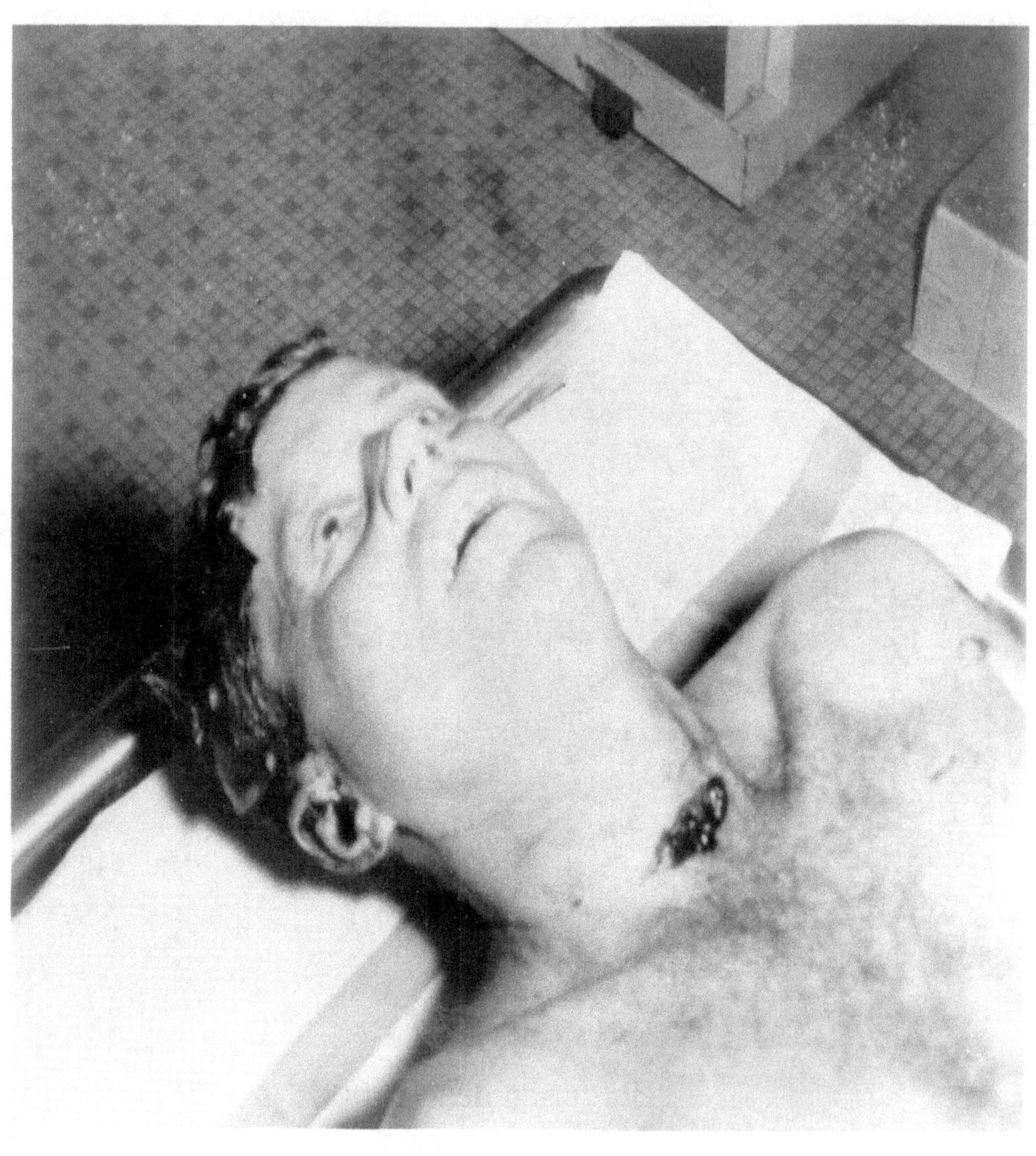

President John F. Kennedy in the morgue.

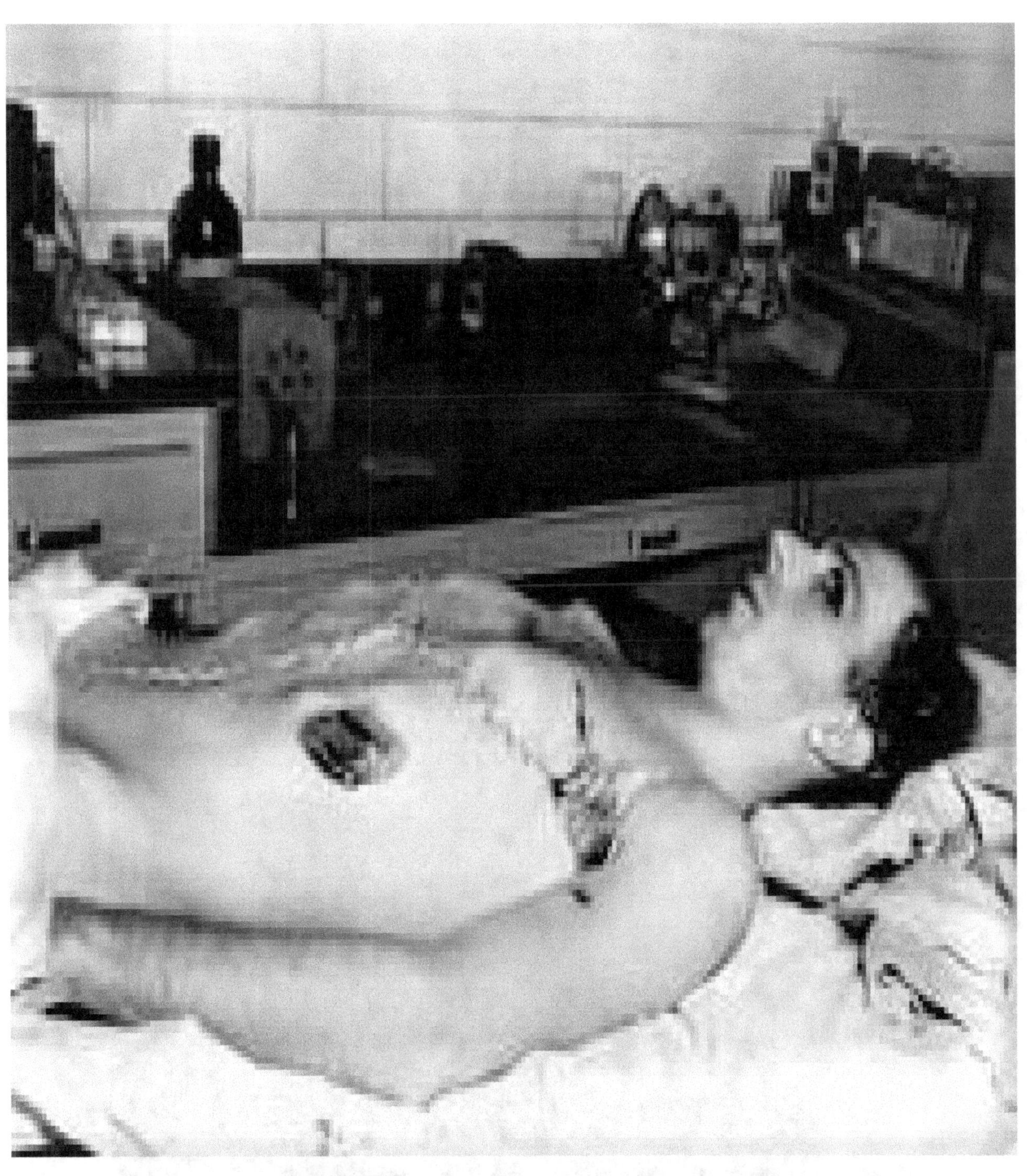

Lee Harvey Oswald the assassin of President Kennedy after autopsy.

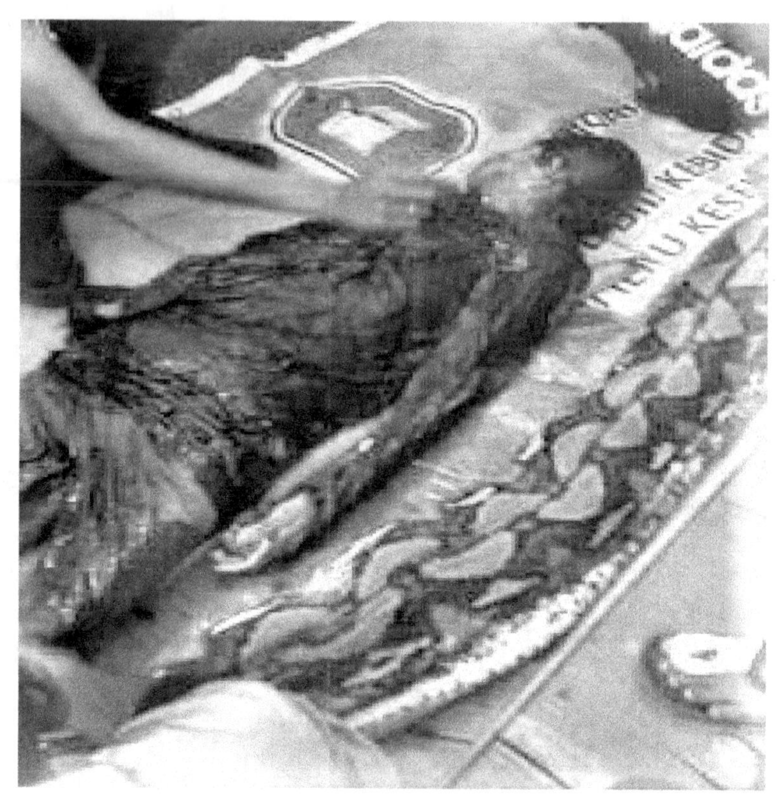

A Woman killed and eaten by a giant python.

STOP!

DID YOU FIND THE FIRST SIX PHOTOGRAPHS UPSETTING?

If the answer is Yes, do not go beyond this point. Close this Book immediately and never open it again!

THE ATROCITIES OF WAR. THE NAZIS.

THE MURDEROUS NAZI DEATH CAMPS

The Nazis built the death camps to depose of humans they dictated as inferior. The victims were in the millions, with a high percentage of Jewish descent. Other races and individuals the Nazis deemed unfit to live, including some POWs, were systematically executed.

As with the Japanese in W.W. 2, the Nazis also used their prisoners in various human experiments. In short, these people were considered vermin, and their suffering was meaningless.

A shortlist of the Nazi experiments include;

Experiments on twins.

Inflicting head injuries and freezing people to death.

Infecting victims with malaria, epidemic jaundice, and other diseases.

Testing mustard gas on the victims.

Sulfonamide experiments.

Seawater experiments.

Bone, muscle, and nerve transplantation.

Sterilization and fertility experiments.

Experiments with poison.

Experiments with incendiary bombs.

High altitude experiments.

Blood coagulation experiments.

Electroshock experiments.

Nazi high-and low-pressure chamber test.   Dachau Camp.

Dr. Joseph Mengele conducted many of the experiments.

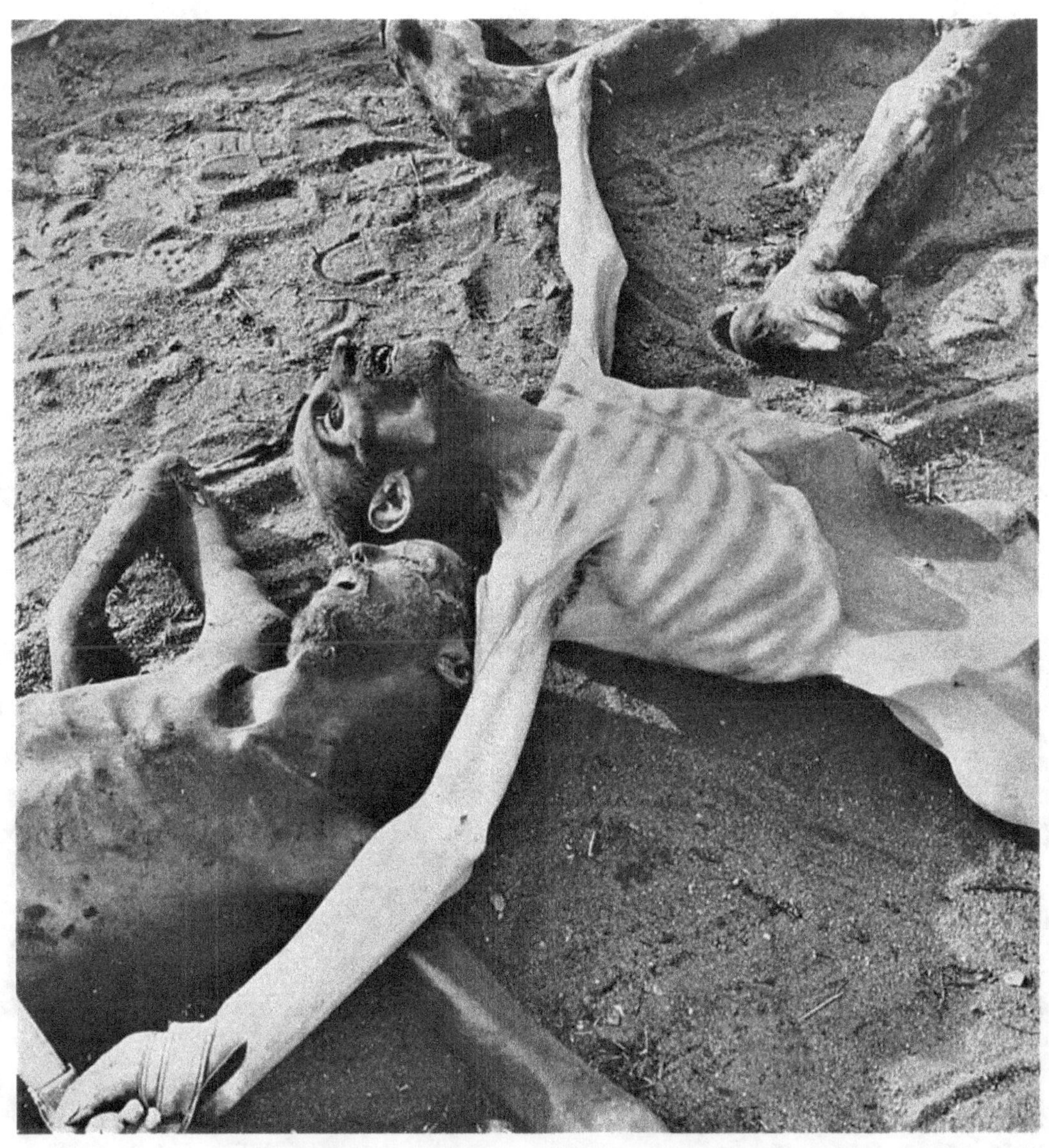

The lives of millions in Nazi death camps ended this way.

The Nazis Buchenwald Concentration Camp.

The world must never forget the millions of innocent people slaughtered by the Nazis.

A once proud German soldier commits suicide—picture of Hitler at his side.

The Nazi Leaders.

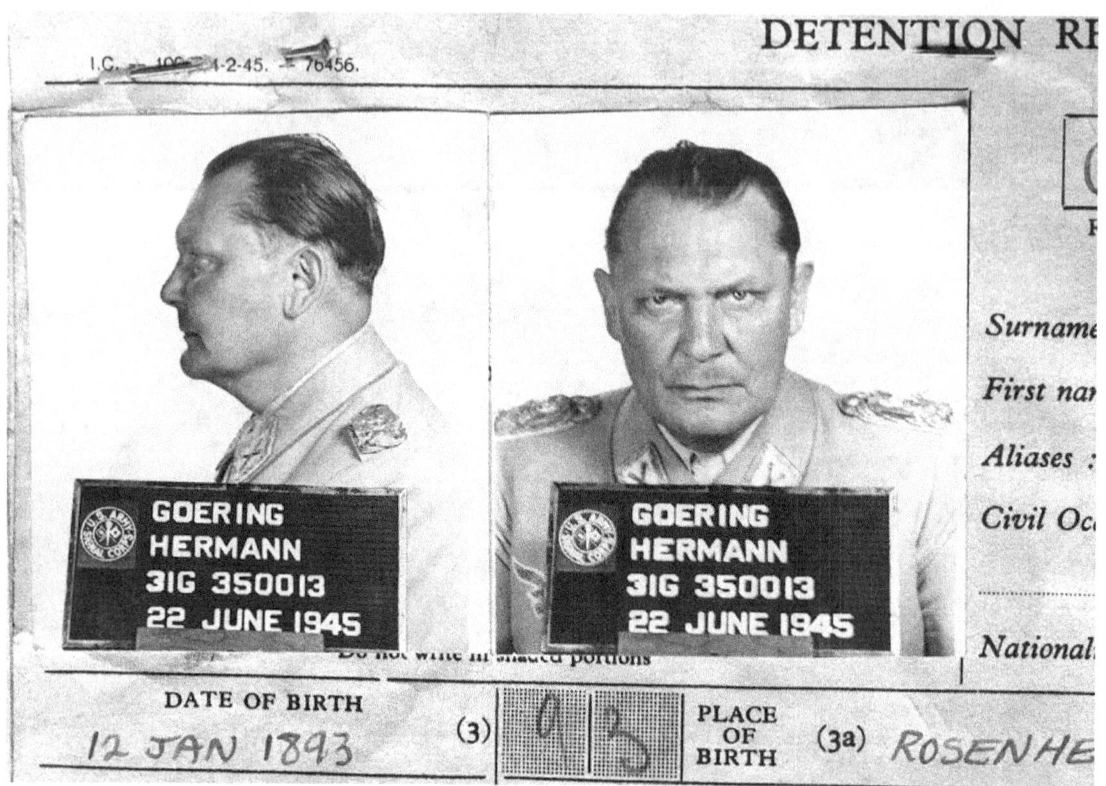

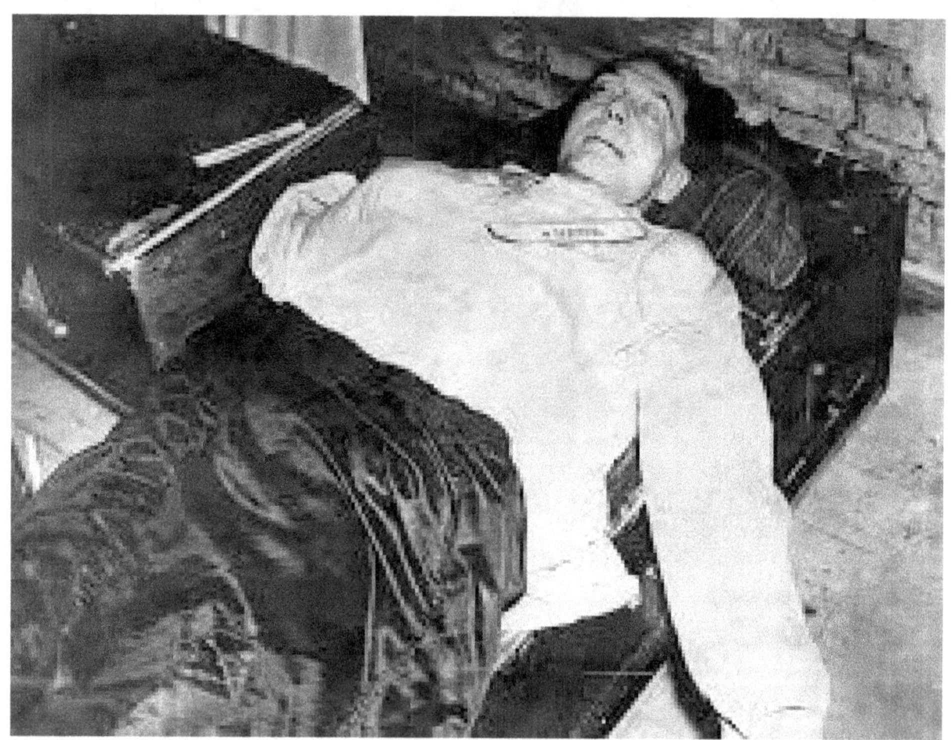

Hermann Goering commits suicide.

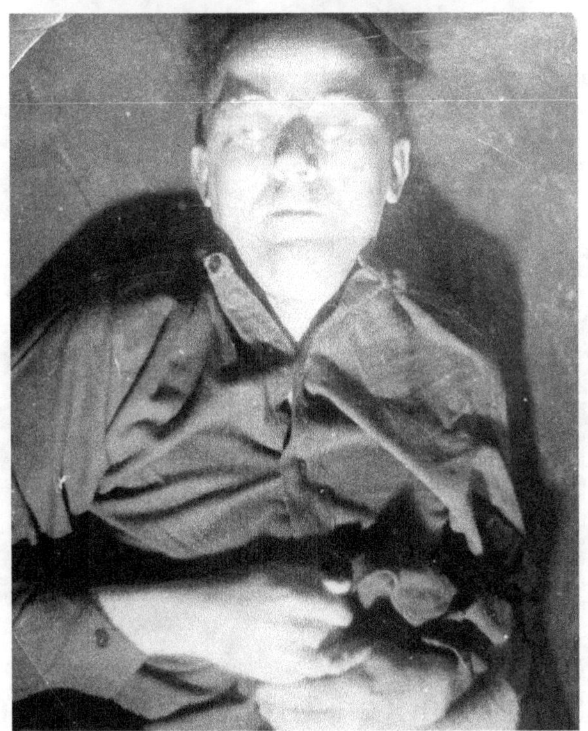

Heinrich Himmler commits suicide.

Joseph Goebbels

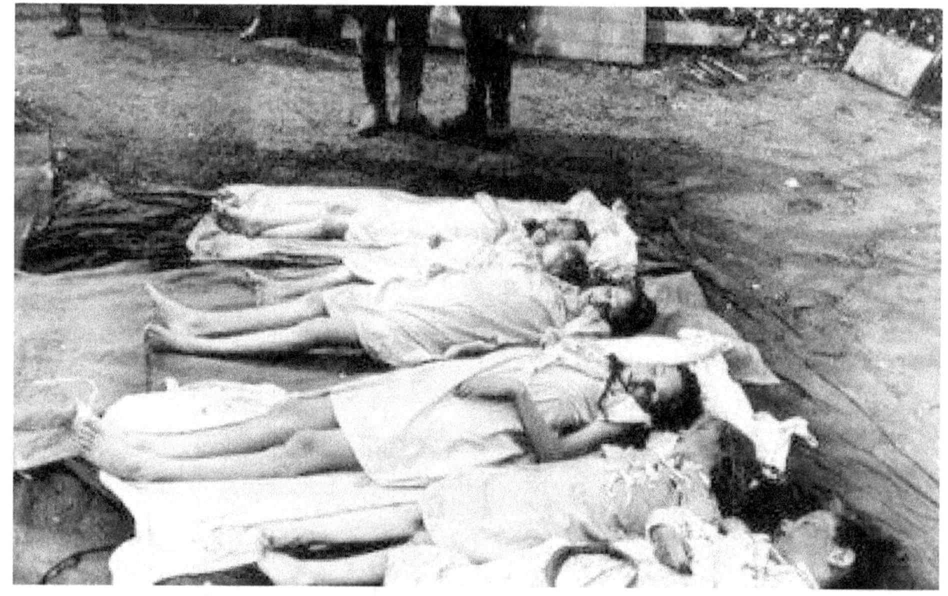

Bodies of Goebbels children after being poisoned by Parents.

Joseph Goebbels and his wife committed suicide and had their bodies burned.

The Murderous Nazi Leader. Adolph Hitler.

Hitler also proved a coward and committed suicide.

Hitler and Eva Braun. They married just before committing suicide.

It's been alleged; this is the ditch where Hitler and Braun's bodies were burned.

Body aflame after Nazi V-2 rocket hit Belgium.
November 27, 1944.

JAPANESE ATROCITIES

DURING

WORLD WAR 2

Australian POW Sergeant Leonard Siffleet seconds before being beheaded by a Japanese soldier. Siffleet and two other commandoes were captured and beheaded on October 24, 1943, by Yasuno Chikao on Aitaoe Beach, New Guinea.

American Forces killed Chikao in April 1944.

Japanese soldier bayonetting a Chinese baby.

W.W. 2 Australian and Dutch POWs being starved by Japanese
1942.

Japanese soldiers burying Chinese civilians alive.

Japanese soldier beheading Chinese civilian.

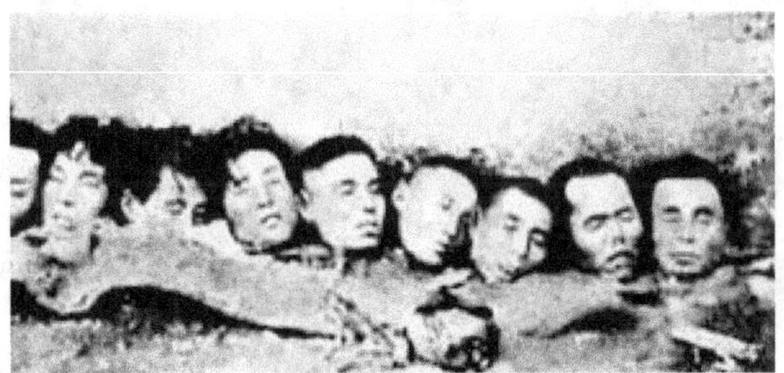

Beheading victims.

Japanese soldiers executing Sikh prisoners.

After being shot, the Sikh prisoners were bayonetted.

Japanese soldiers practiced bayoneting live Chinese civilians.
It was considered a "Test of Courage" for the soldiers.

Background of Japan's Infamous Unit 731

During World War 2, the Japanese and Nazis performed brutal and predominantly fatal experiments on their POWs and civilians.

Some of the human experiments carried out at 731 include;

Vivisections on men, women, and children without anesthesia; the vast majority died.

Biological research by infecting the victims with various fatal and non-fatal diseases.

Weapon testing; tying live people to poles, then shooting them with various weapons, setting off grenades at multiple distances to view the impact on a live person, testing flamethrowers on live victims, and testing bayonets and knives on men, women, and children.

They determined how long it would take to die from lack of water or food.

Determining the Length of Time to die from lethal x-rays

Injecting animal blood and seawater into the living

Spinning people to death in a centrifuge.

Killing people in high-and low-pressure chambers.

Winter testing included allowing body parts to freeze and tying people to poles in freezing weather to determine how long it took to freeze to death.

Infecting people with syphilis, then forcing them to have sex. Once the male and female tested positive, they underwent vivisections at various stages of the disease.

Lt. Gen. Shiro Ishii
Commander of Unit 731

The infamous Japanese Unit 731 conducting a human experiment.

Spraying a Chinese child with an unknown chemical.

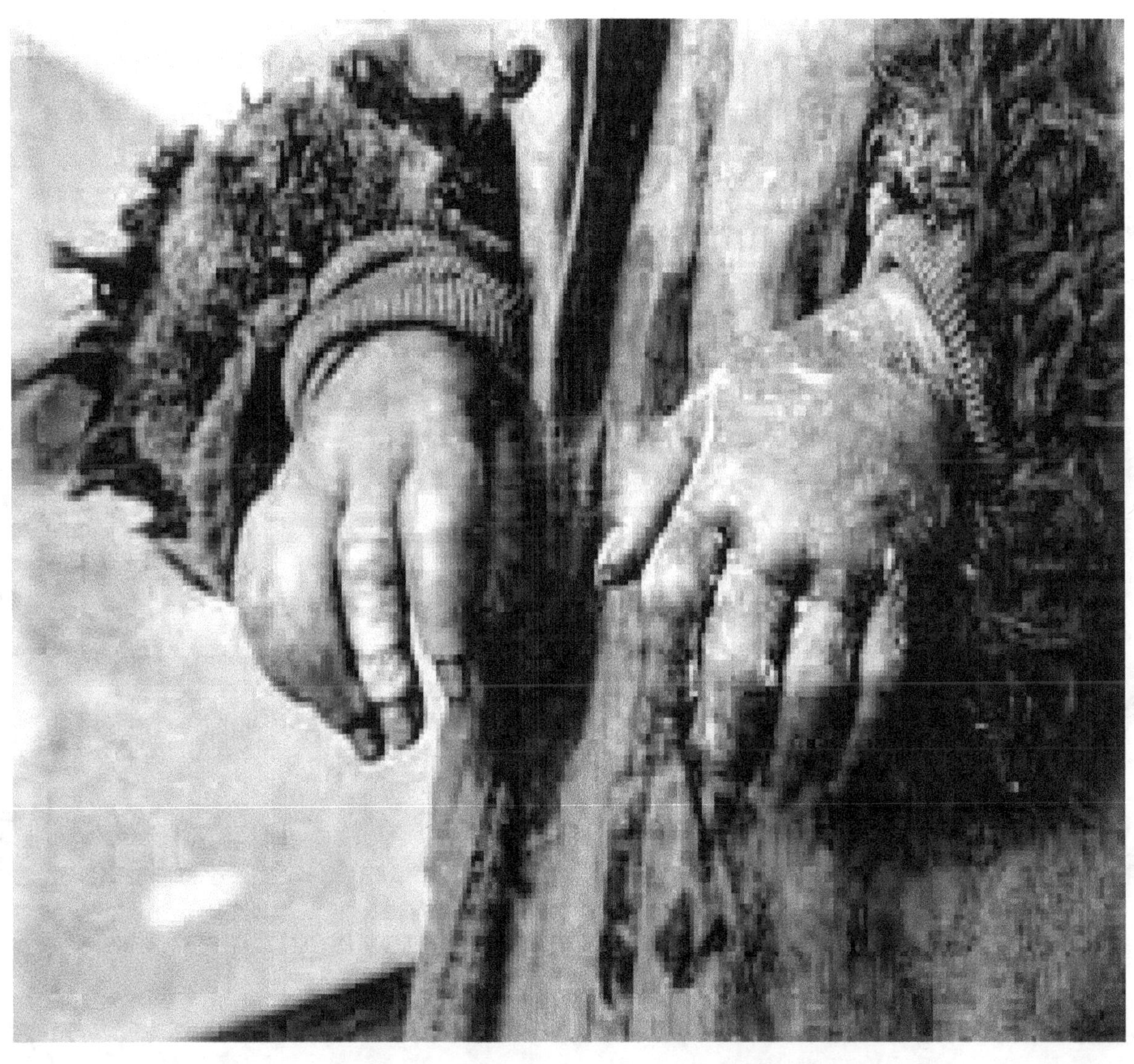

Victim of Unit 731. Victim's hands were frozen to Study frostbite.

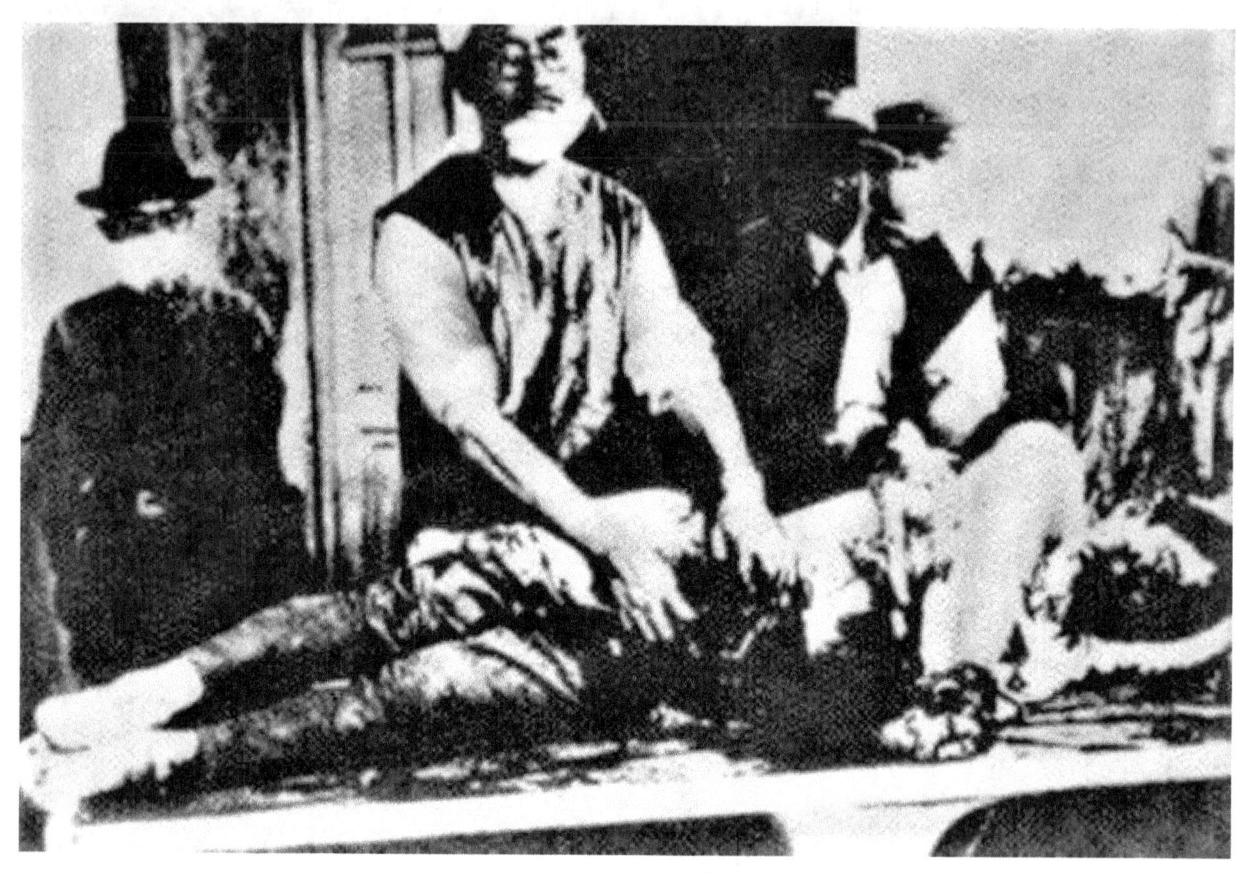

Japanese Doctor performing vivisection.

Victims lashed to a pole for an experiment.

A Despicable Contest Praised in the Japanese Press.

The December 13, 1937 story in the Tokyo "Nichi Shimbun's" details a Contest to kill 100 Chinese using a Sword. Lt. Mukai (left) and Lt. Noda (right).

The Headline reads, "Incredible Record"—Mukai 106 and Noda 105. Both 2nd Lieutenants Go Into Extra Innings."

After the war, a written record of the contest was located and given to the Far East International Military Tribunal. Soon after, the two soldiers were extradited to China, tried by the Nanjing War Crimes Tribunal, convicted of atrocities committed during the Battle of Nanjing and the subsequent massacre. On January 28, 1948, both soldiers were executed at the Yuhuatai Execution Chamber by the Chinese government.

Noda said they did have a contest, but he did not kill that many.

The Japanese slaughtered countless Chinese civilians during their invasion of Nanjing in 1937.

The victims line the banks of the Quinhuai River China.

Burned Japanese soldier. Engebi Island 1944.

Heads on display after a massive beheading.

Chinese children massacred by the Japanese.

Another Japanese soldier beheads a prisoner.

A smiling Japanese soldier holding the head of a person, he just beheaded.

AMERICAN CIVIL WAR INJURIES.

Jacob Miller was shot between the eyes during the Civil War.

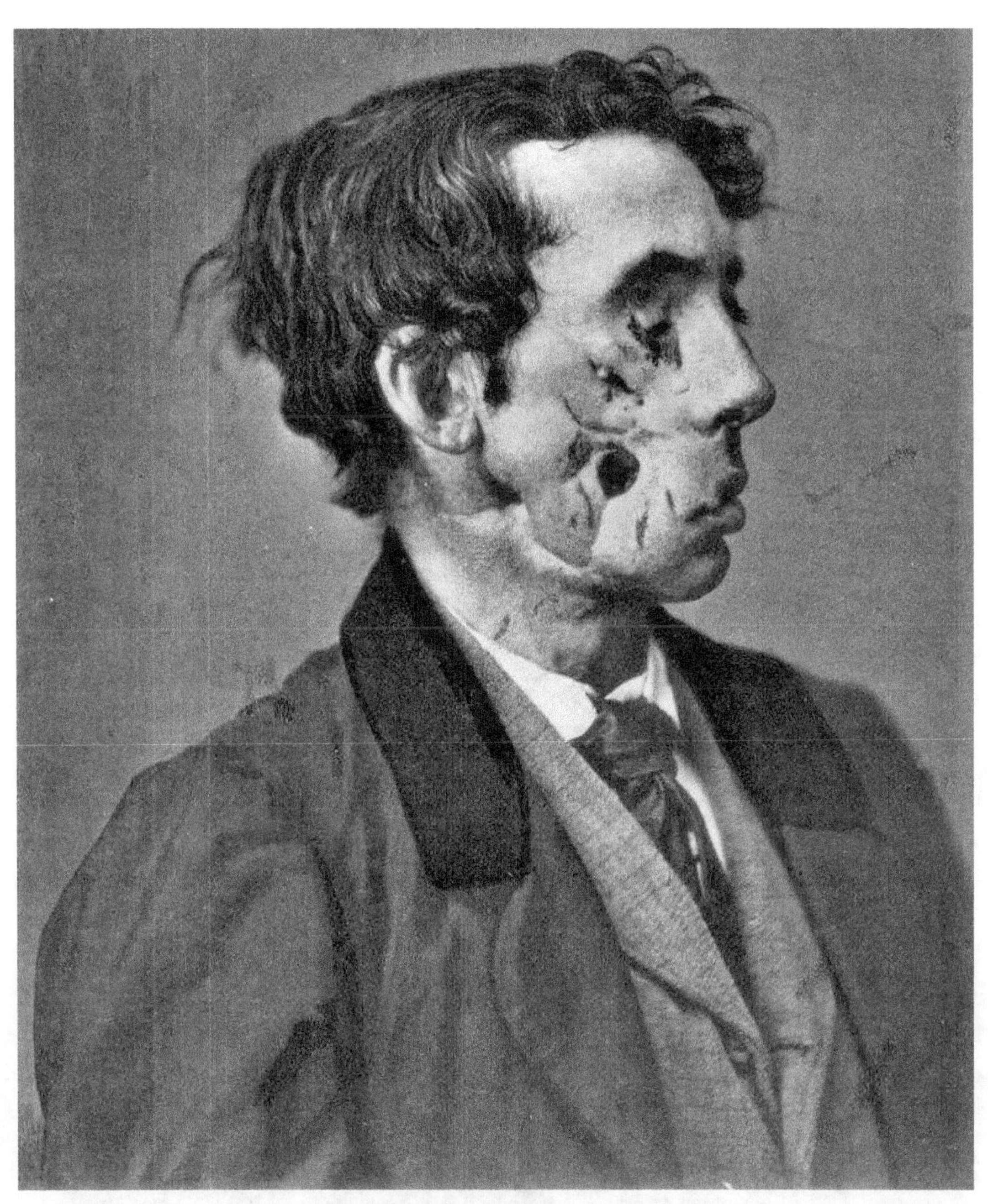

Civil War.

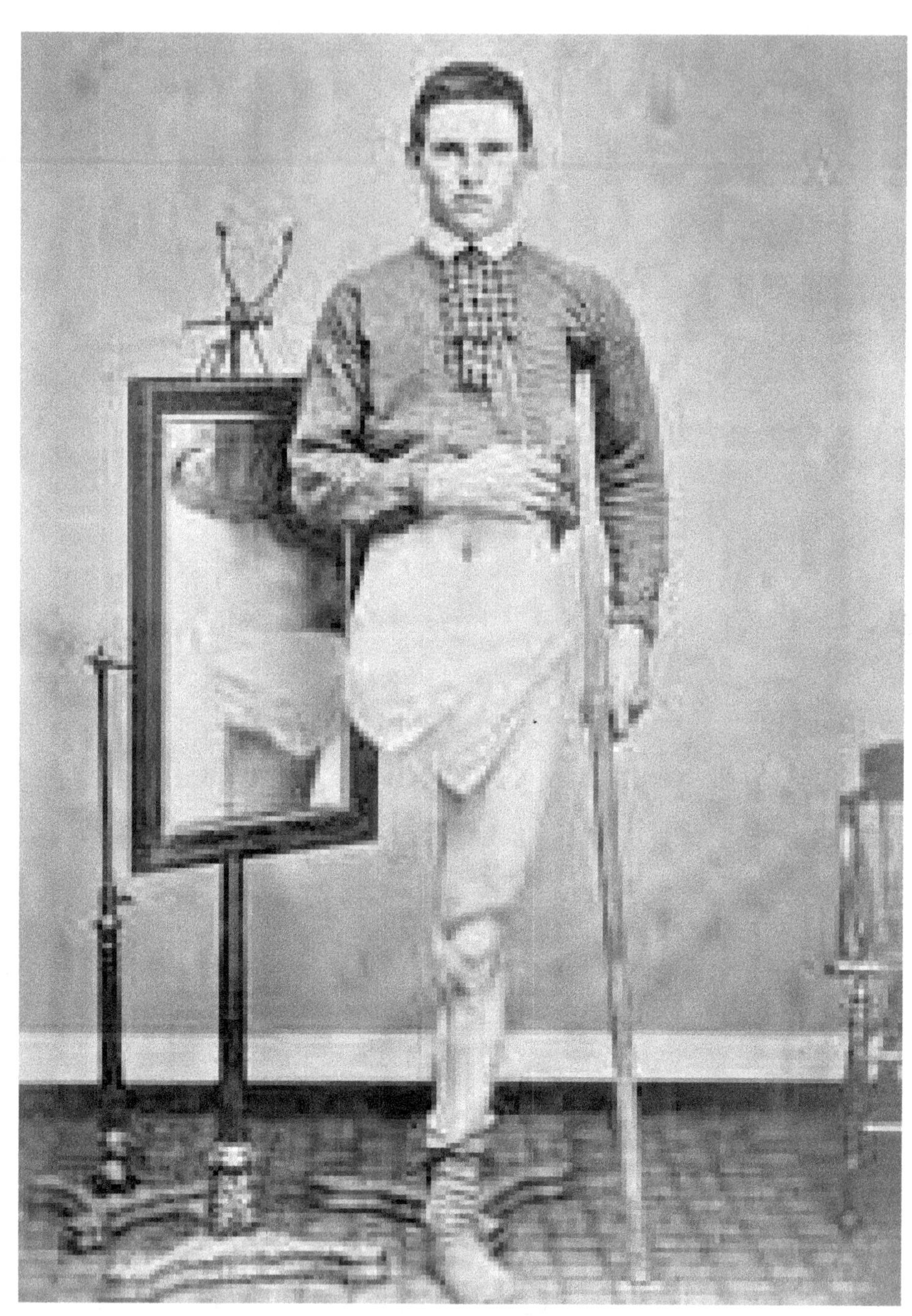

Civil War.

Civil War.

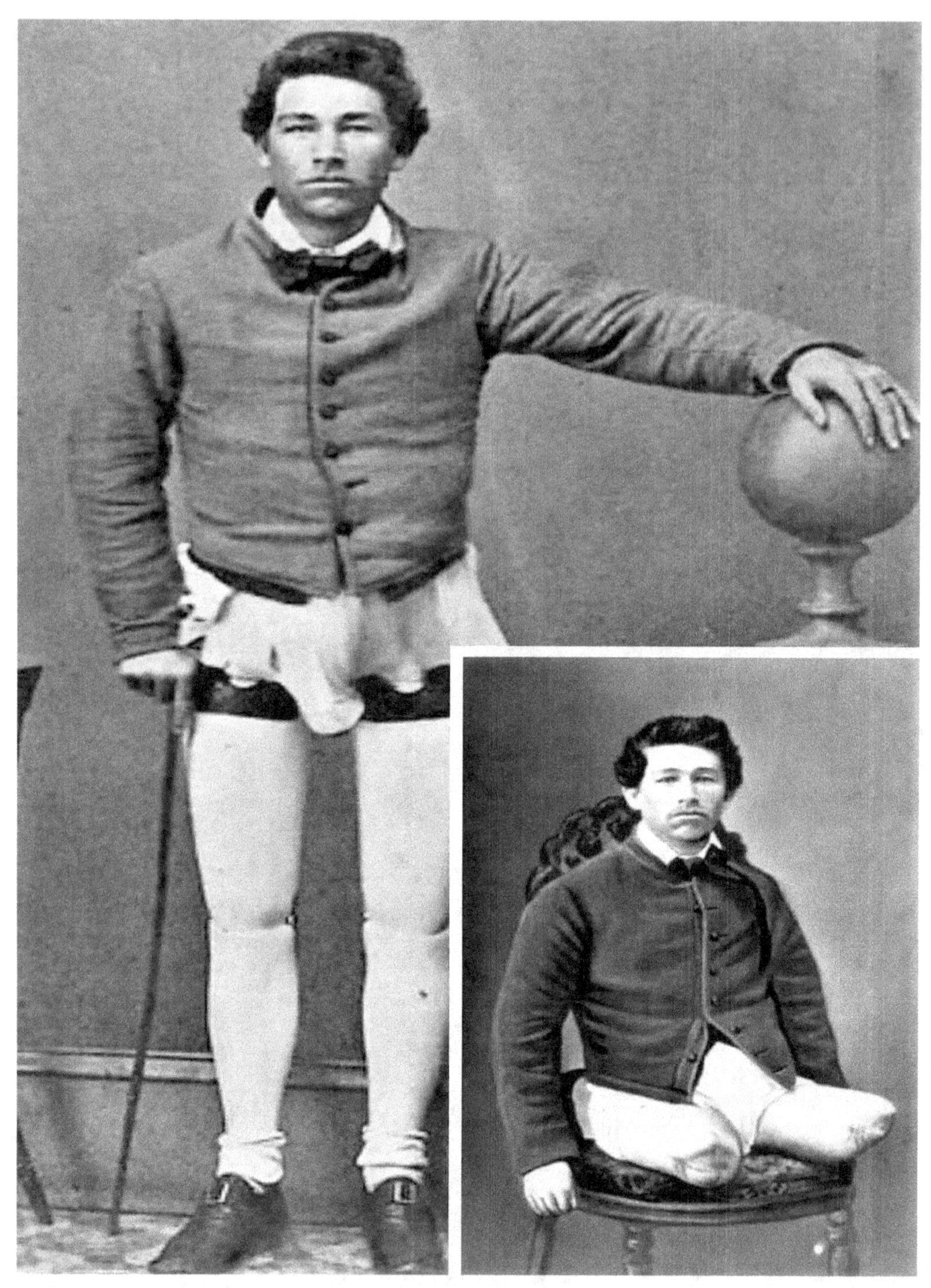

Civil War.

Recovering the remains at Cold Harbor battle site.

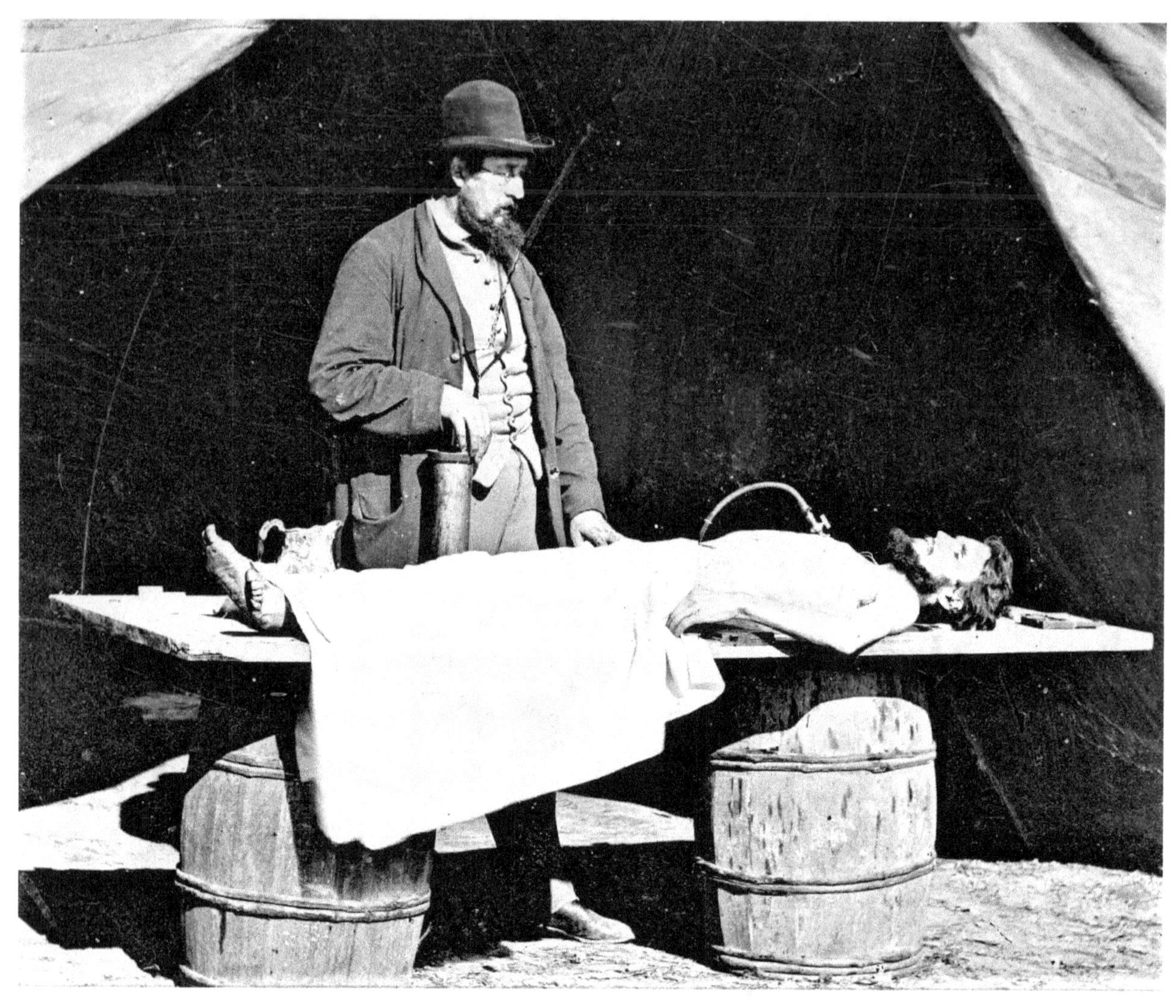

Embalming a soldier during the Civil War.

WORLD WAR 1 INJURIES.

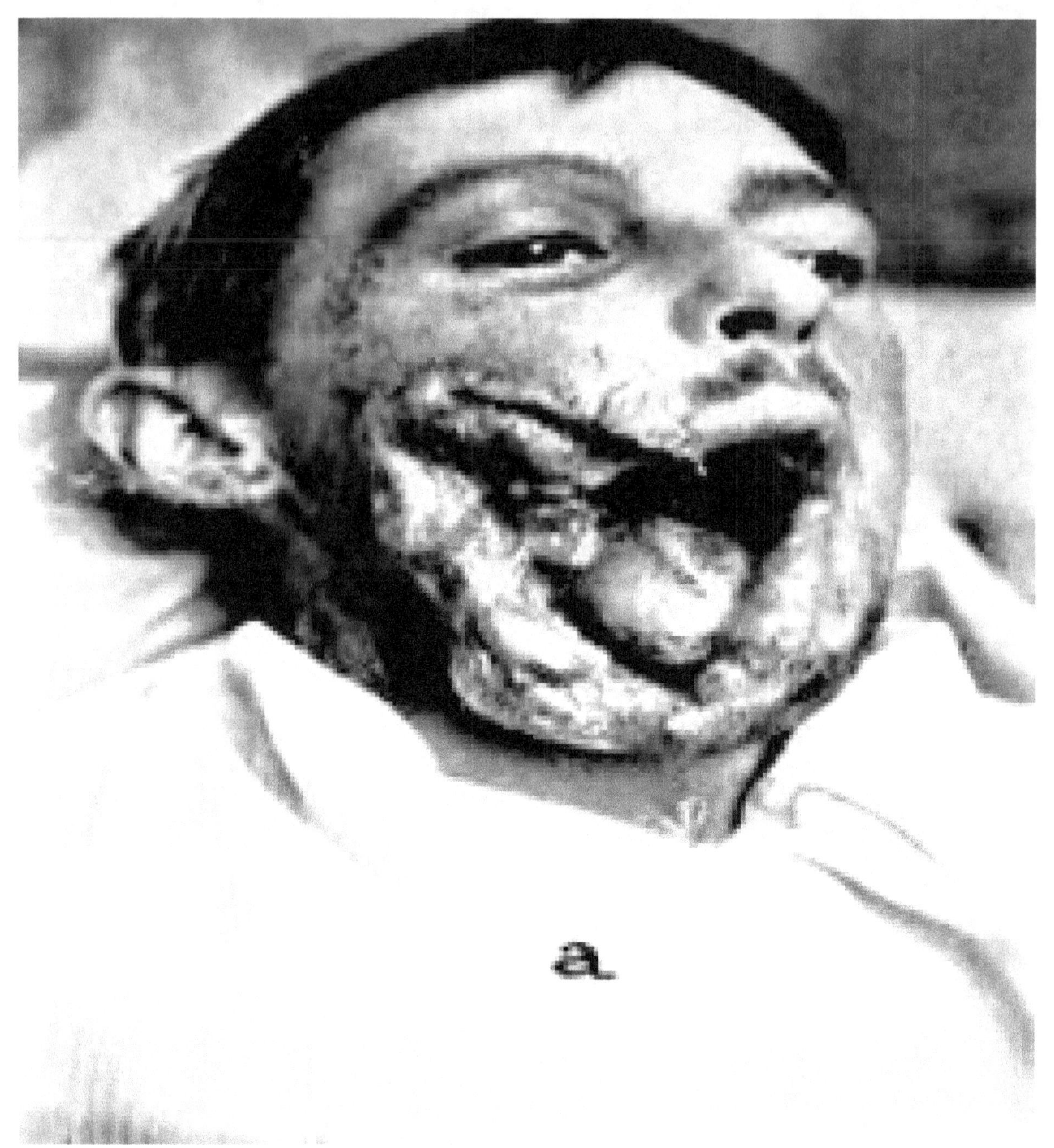

World War 1.

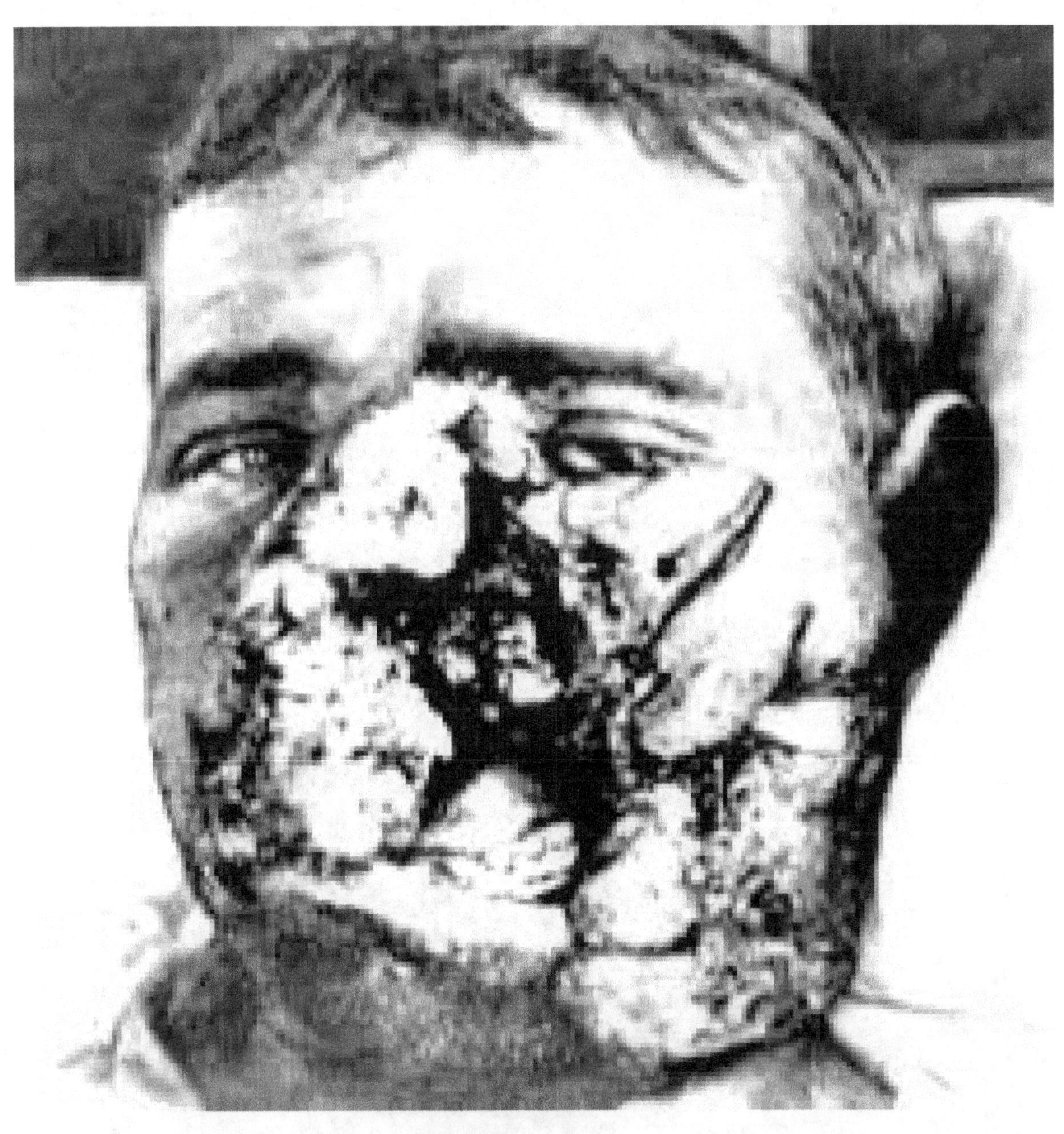

World War 1.

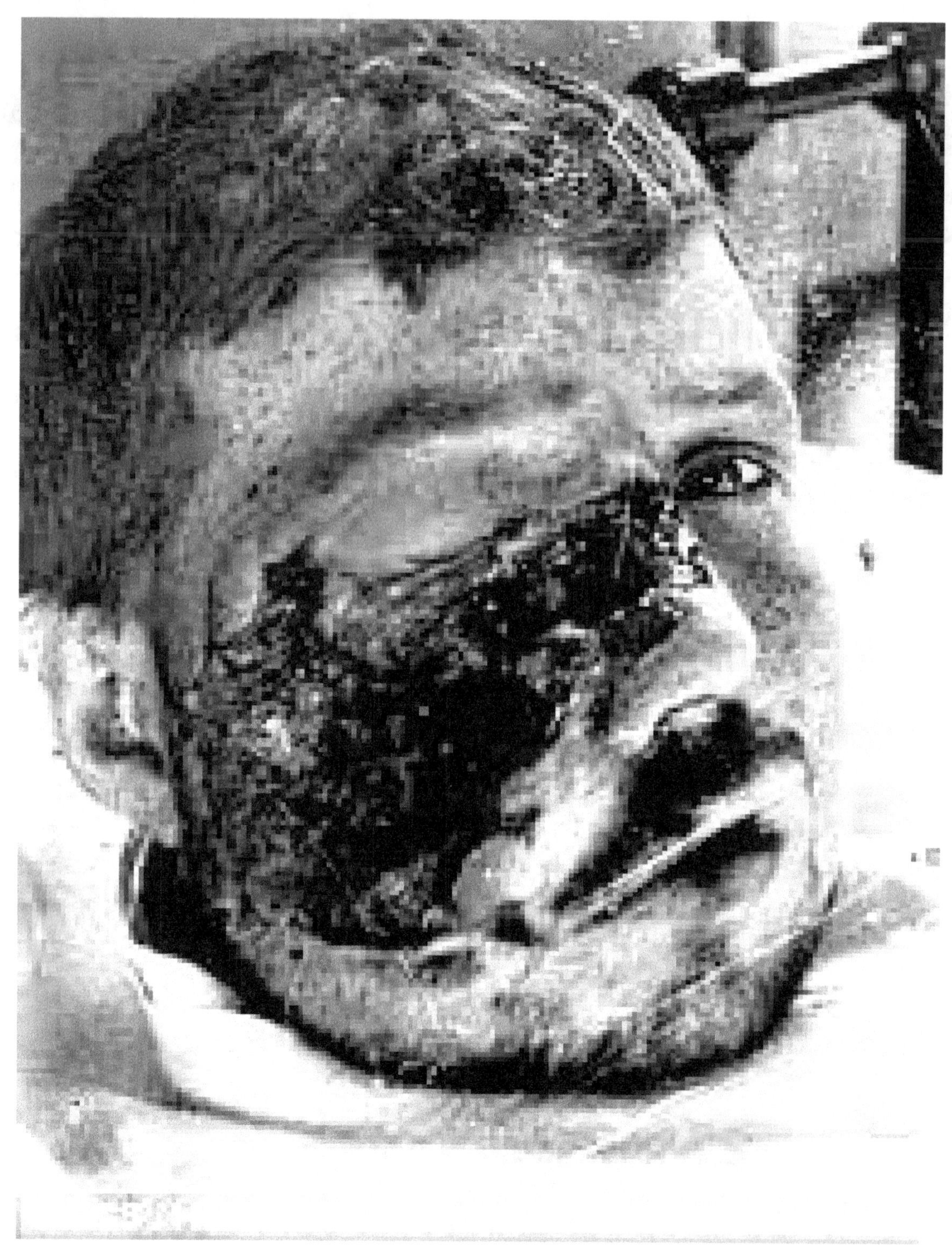

World War 1.

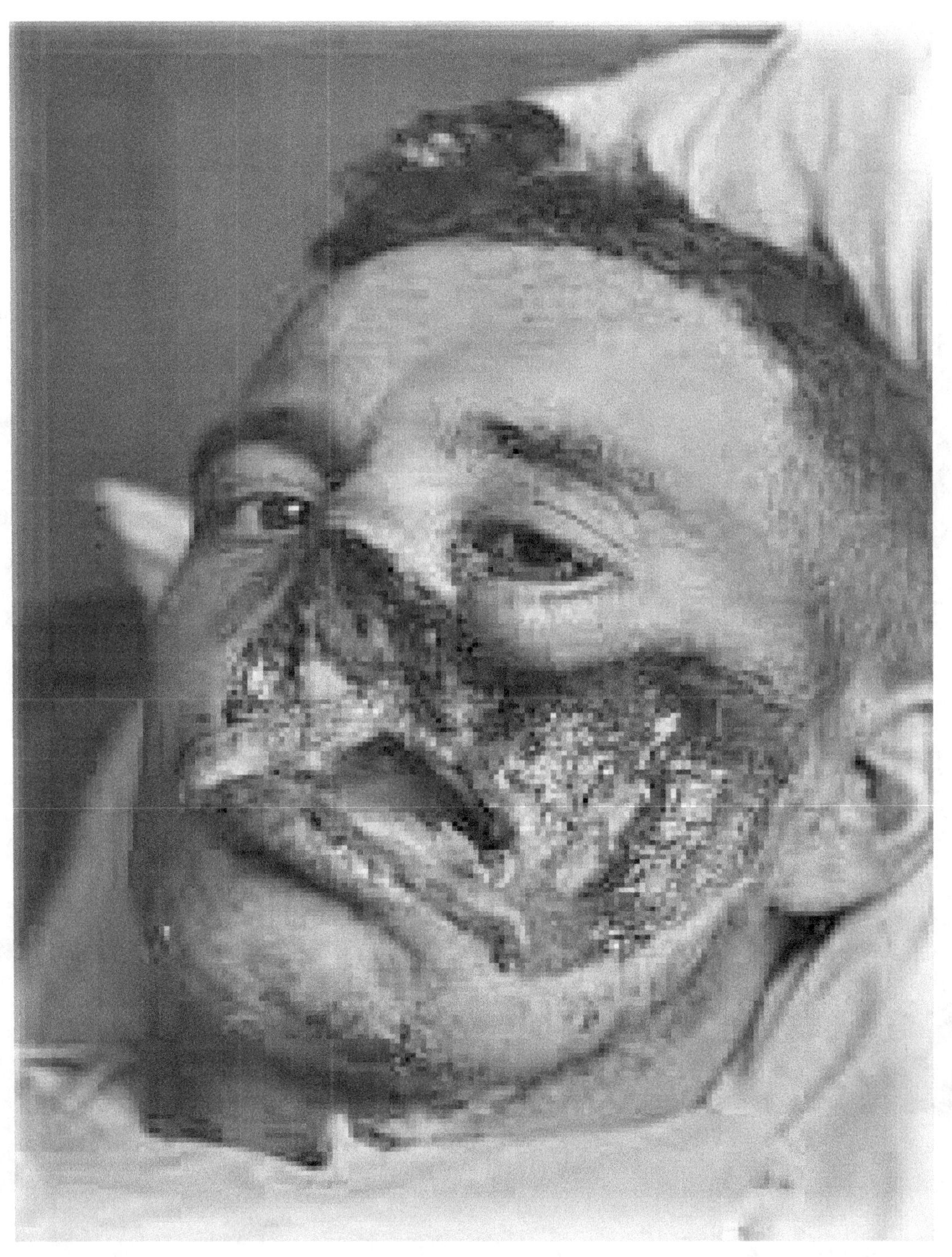

World War 1.

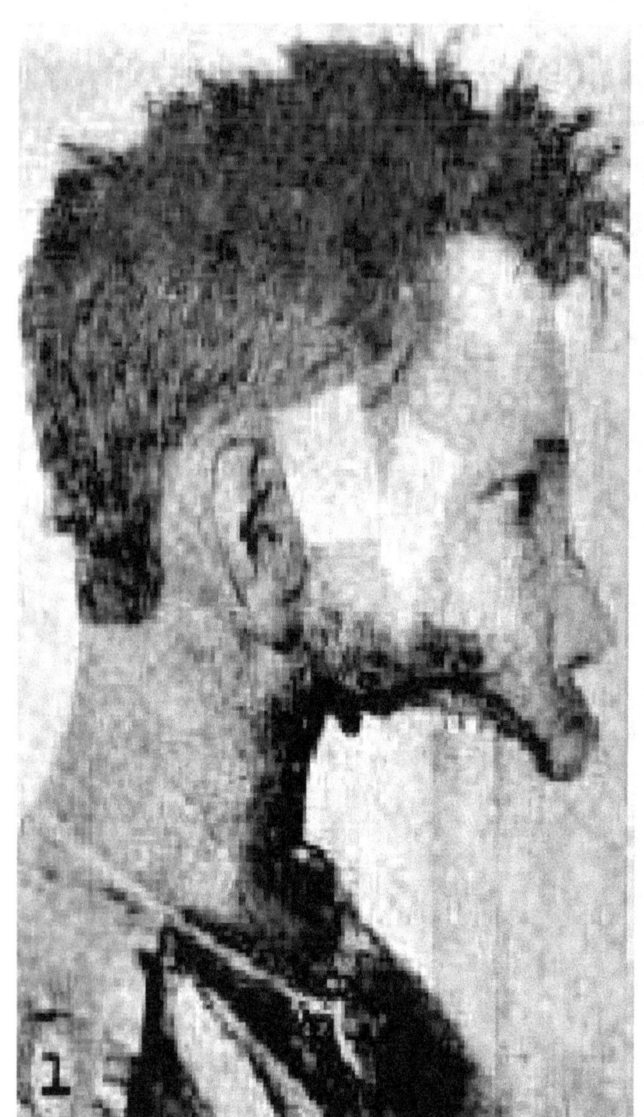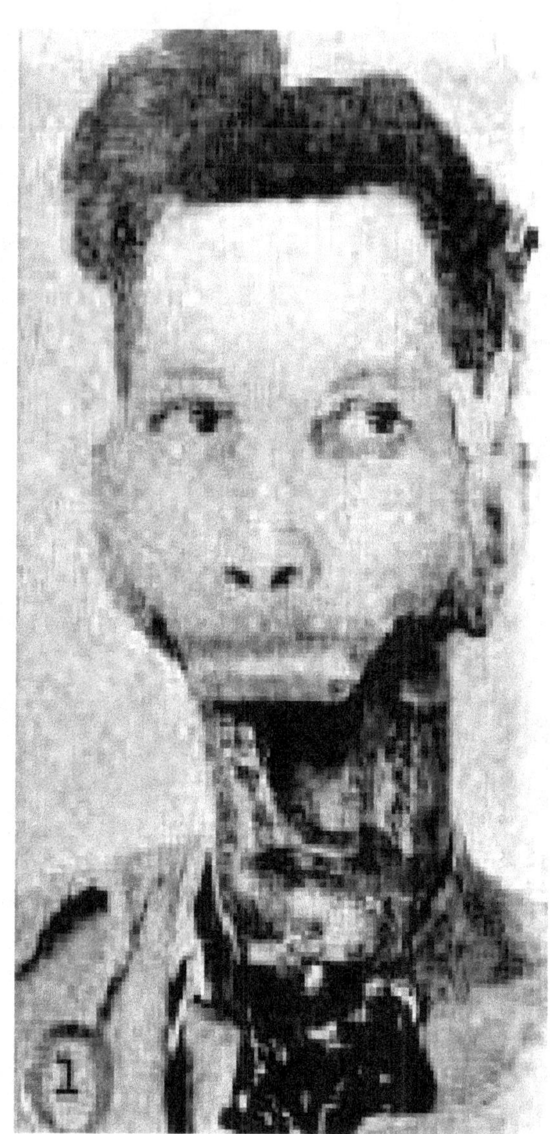

World War 1.

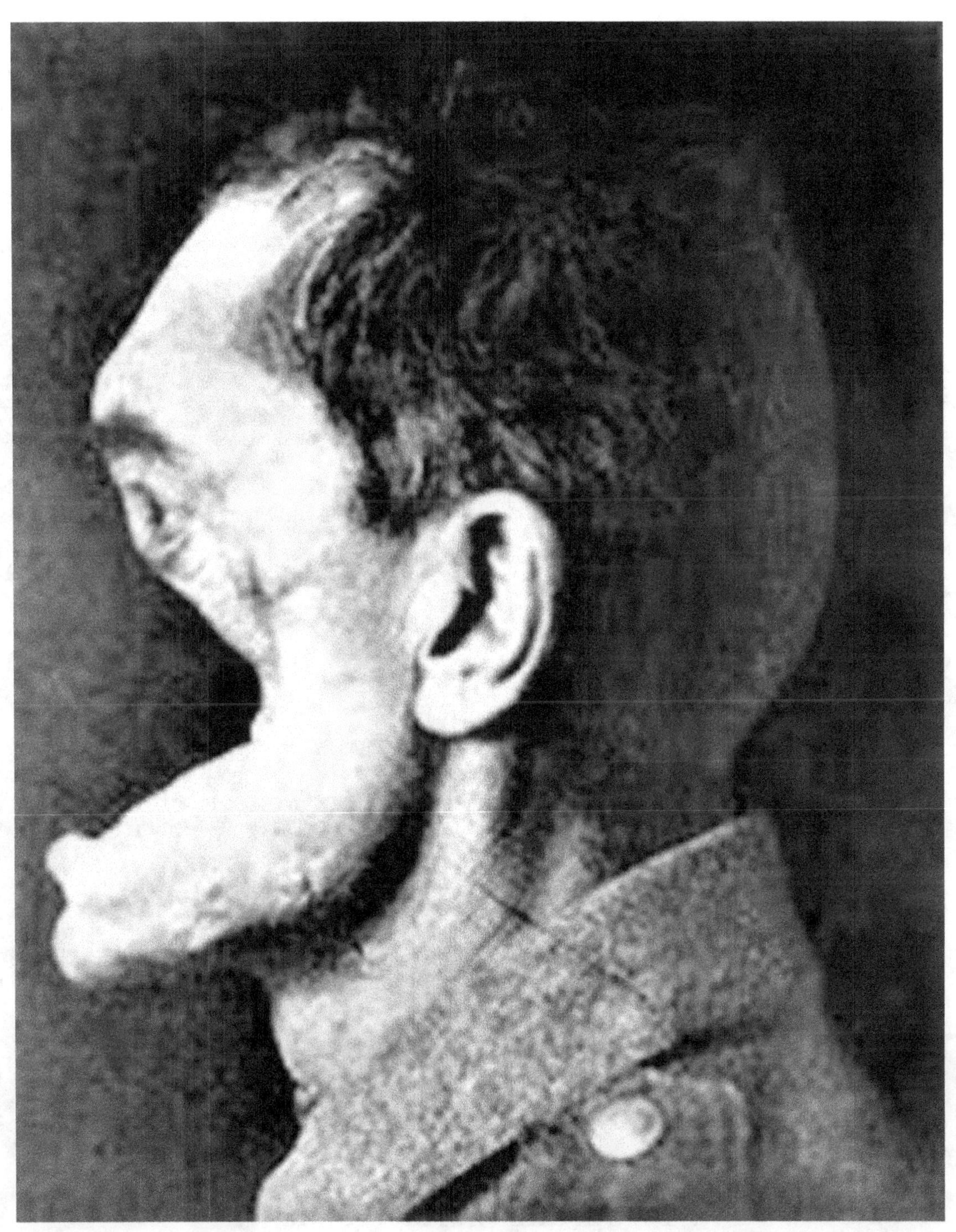

World War 1.

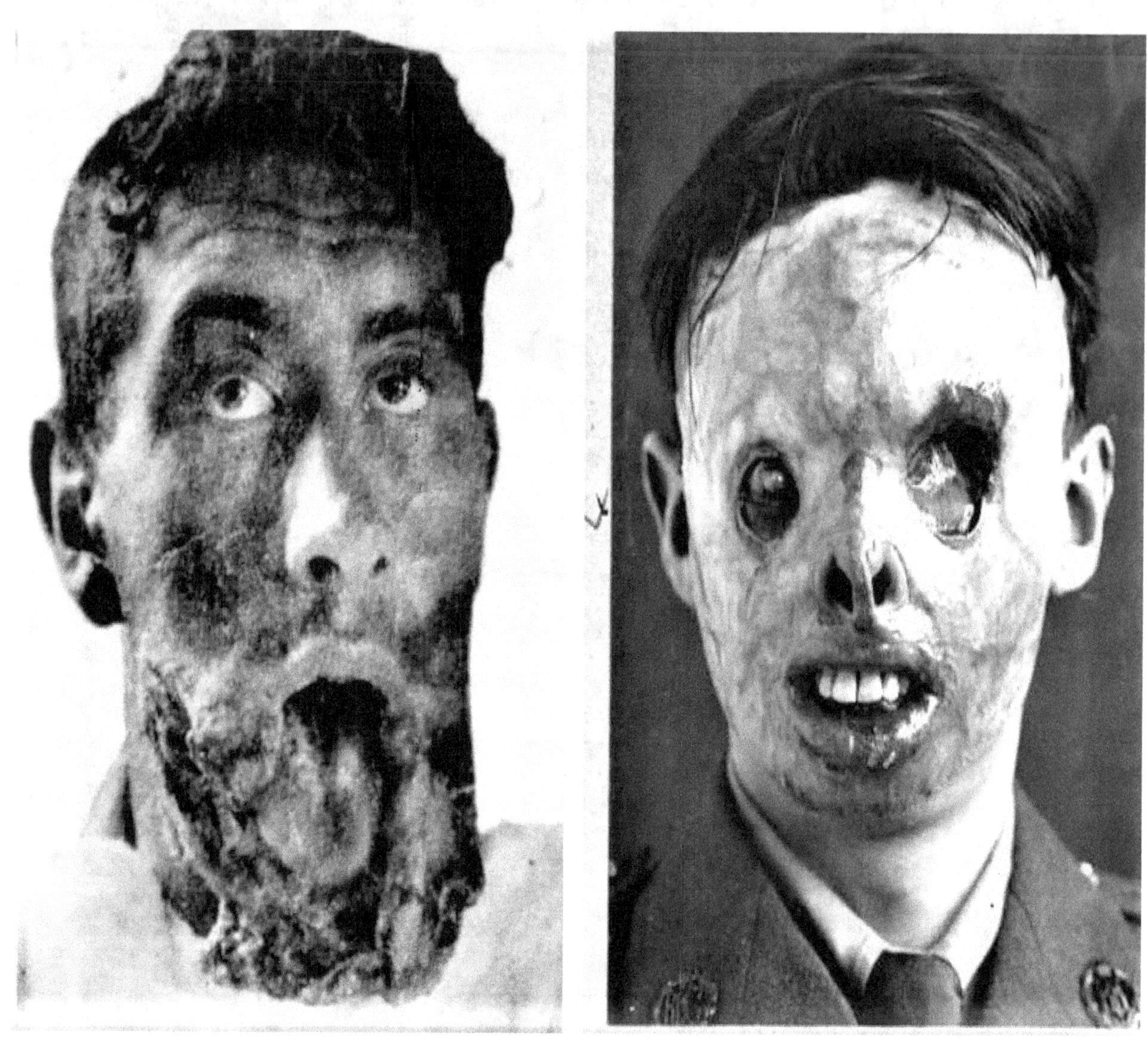

Two from World War 1.

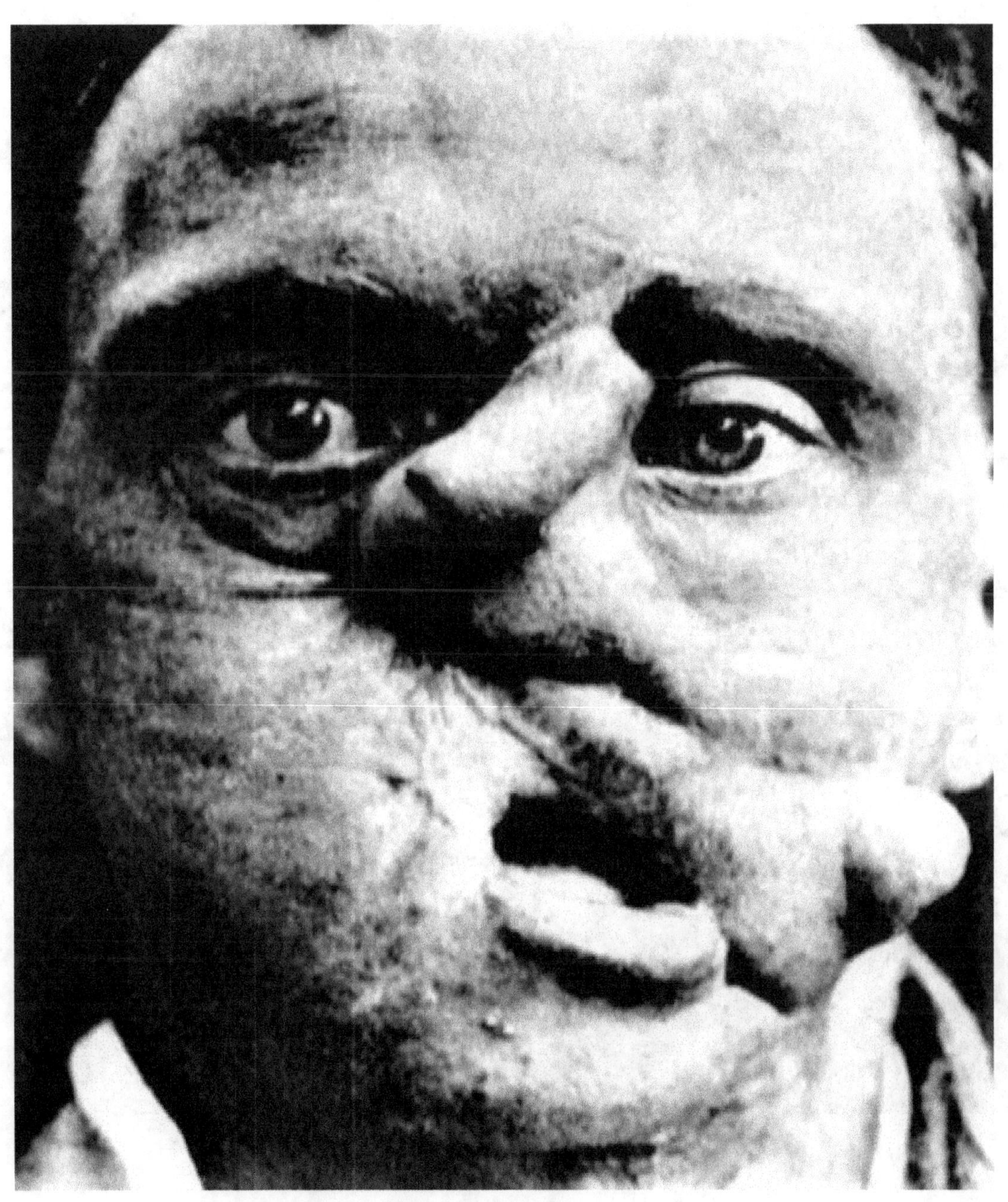

World War 1.

Remains of a German soldier

World War 1.

Remains of a German soldier

World War 1.

Bodies decompose in the trenches of World War 1.

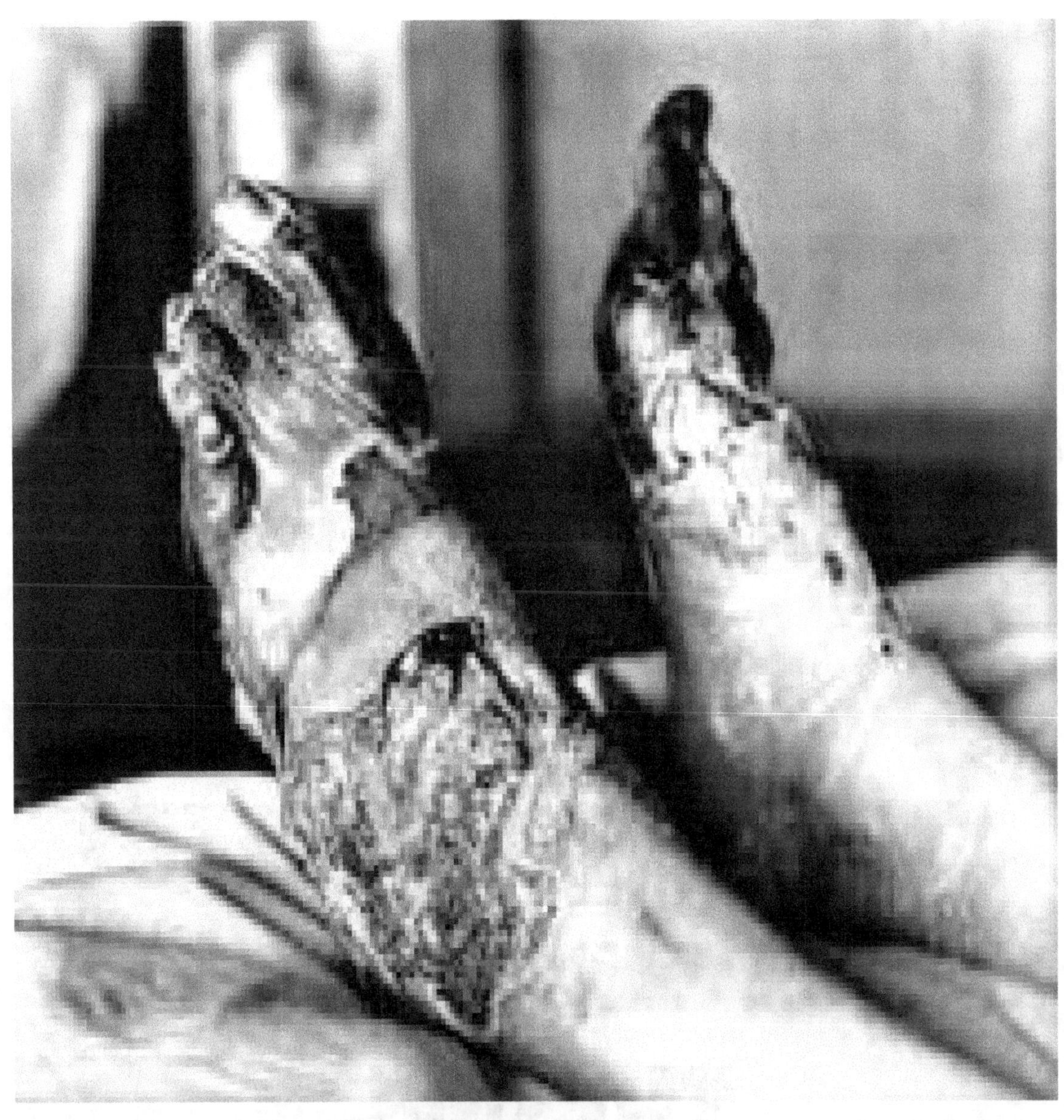

World War 1.

Trench foot, also known as immersion foot, occurs when the feet are wet for long periods. Countless soldiers suffered from this during the war as their feet rotted.

THE BIZARRE, CRIME, AND WTF'S?

FIRST, THE MOBSTERS LIVE BY THE GUN, DIE BY THE GUN.

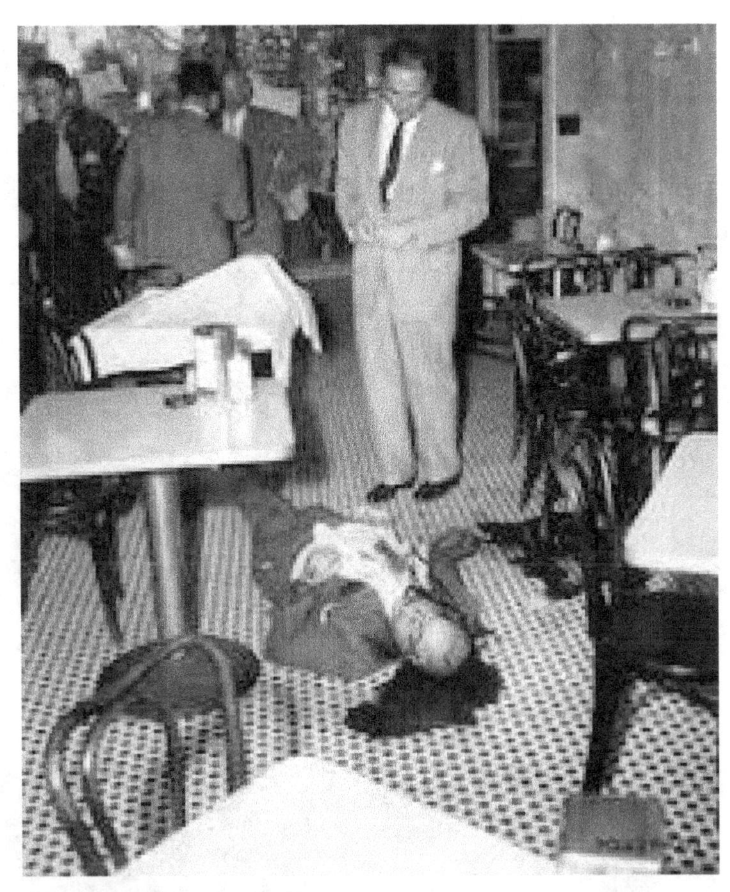

He didn't leave a tip!

Bugsy Siegel

Bugsy during healthier times.

Coca-Cola
ICE COLD

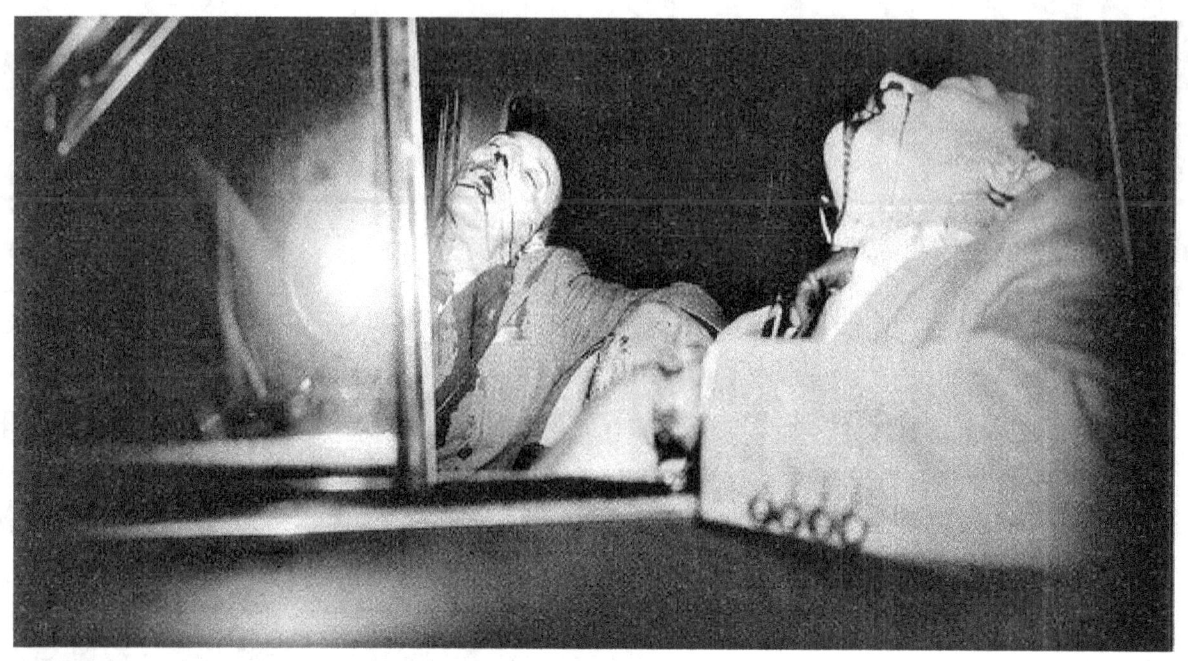

St. Valentine's Day Massacre. Al Capone's men killed seven of the Bugs
Moran gang.
Chicago 1929

THAT IS ENOUGH ABOUT MOBSTERS.

NOW,
THE OUTLAWS.

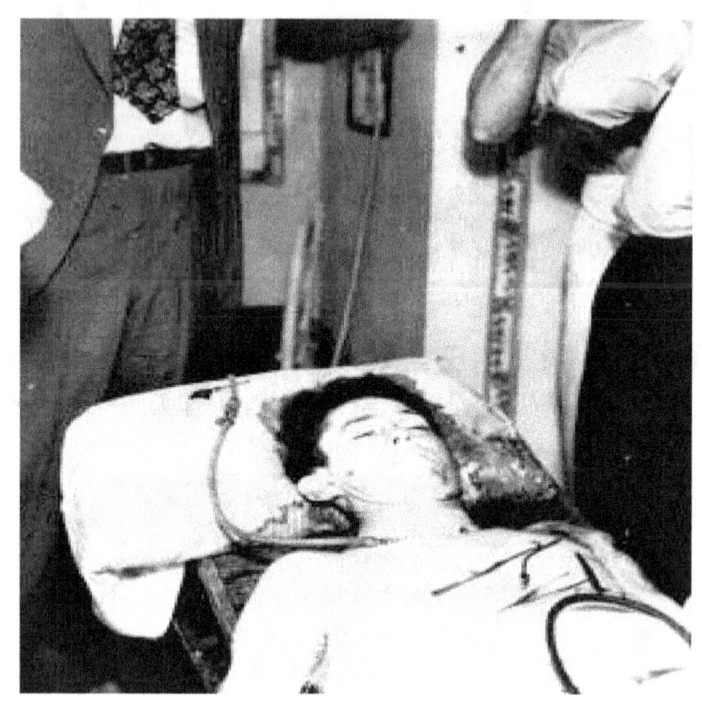

Outlaw Clyde Barrow being embalmed.
Bonnie and Clyde dead.

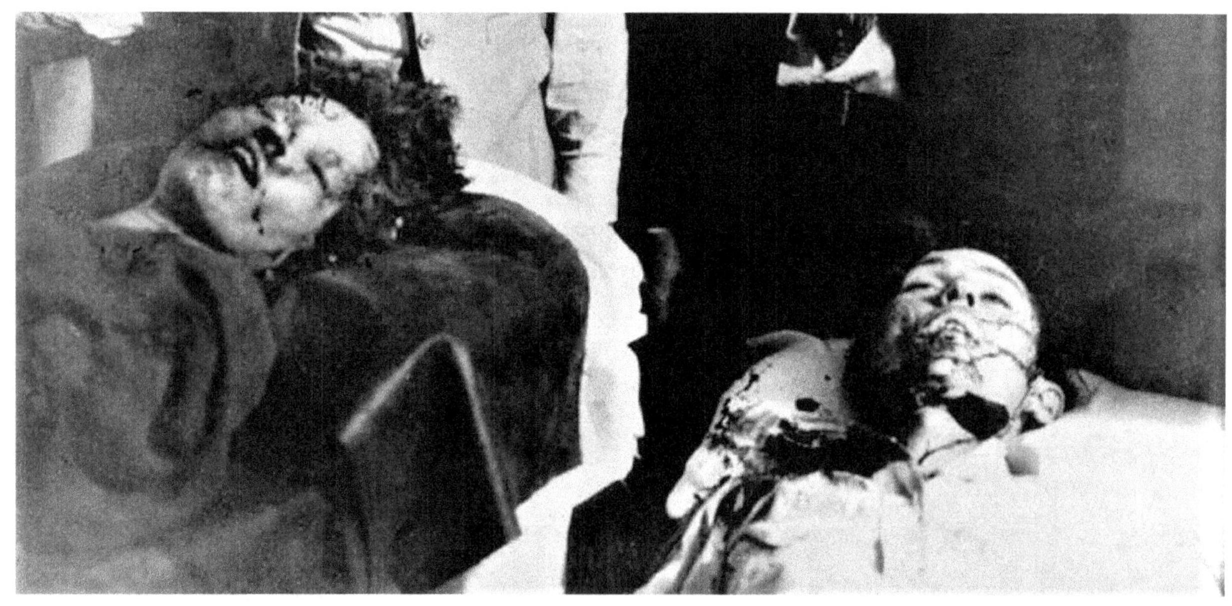

Bonnie and Clyde's car with their bodies inside.

Bonnie and Clyde in happier times.

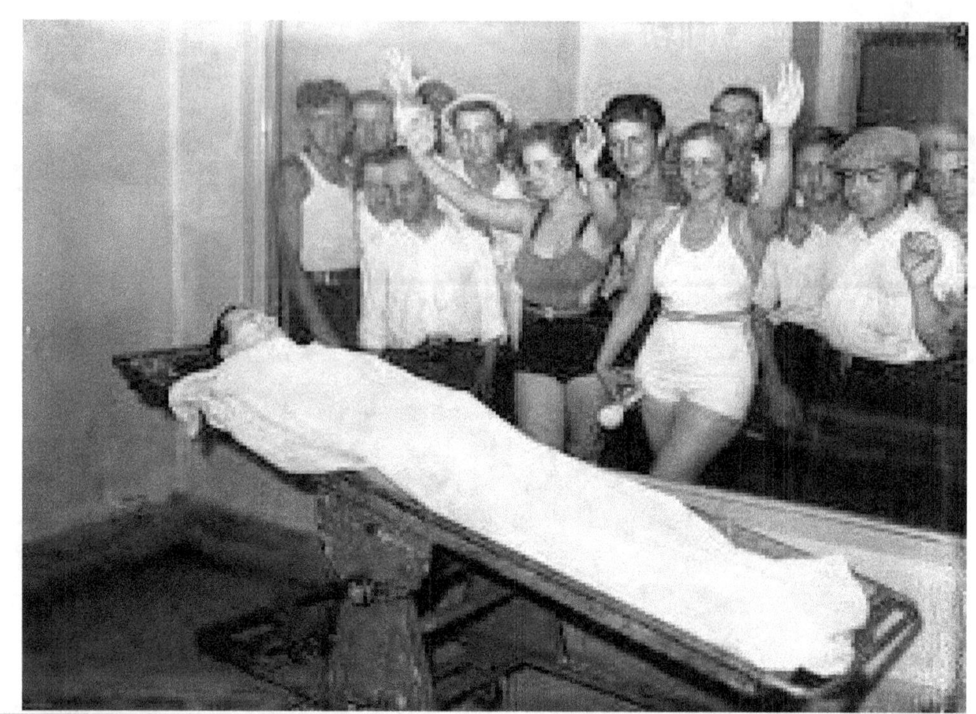

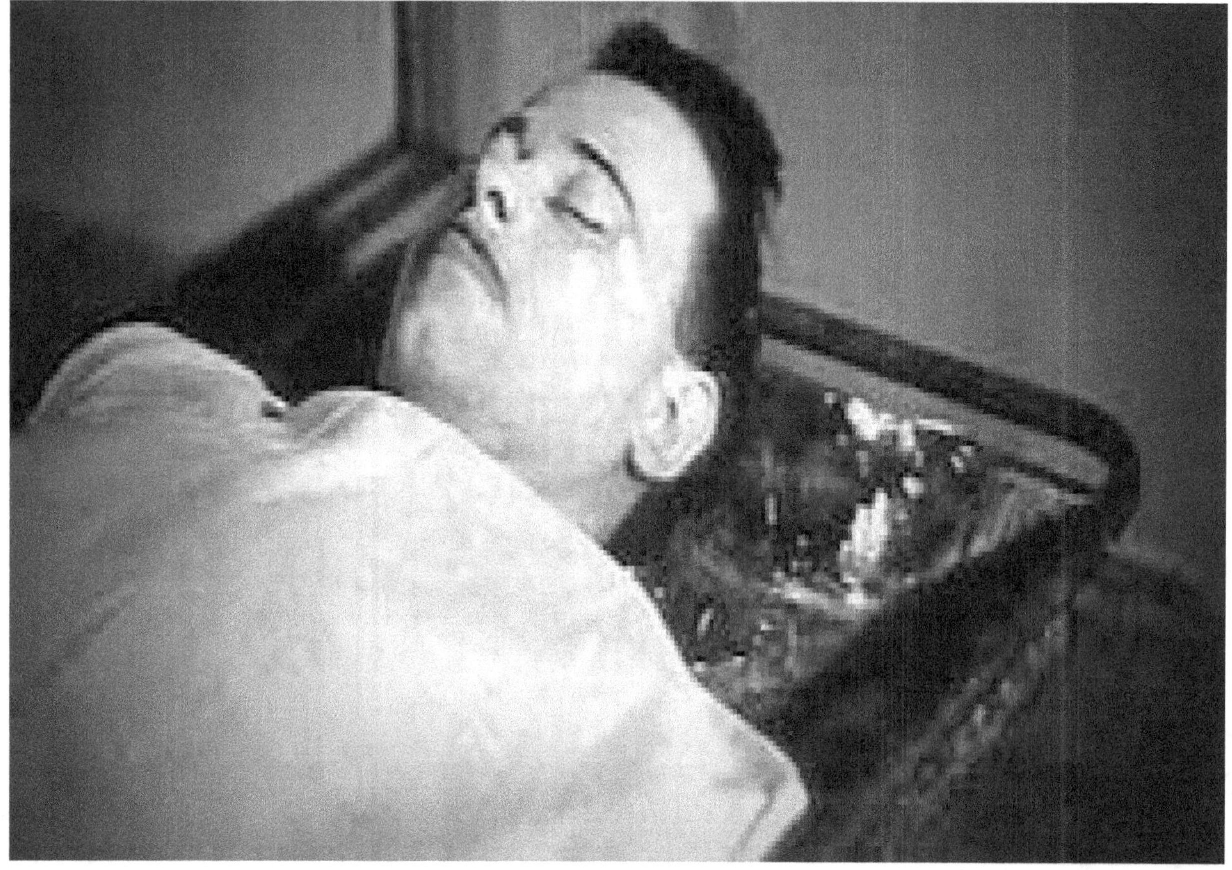

John Dillinger

Above and below.

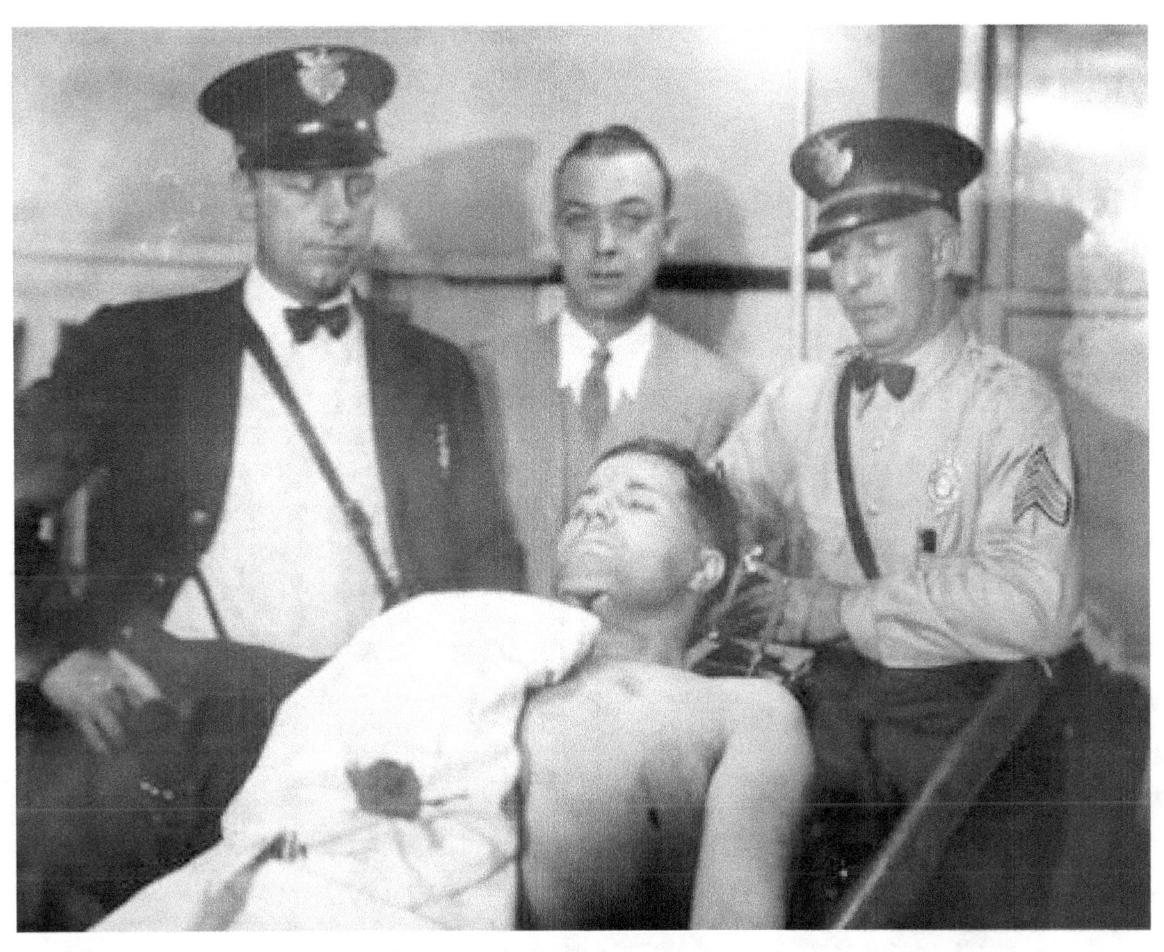

Charles Arthur Floyd **AKA** "Pretty Boy Floyd."

Above and below.

Dead outlaws and cowboys

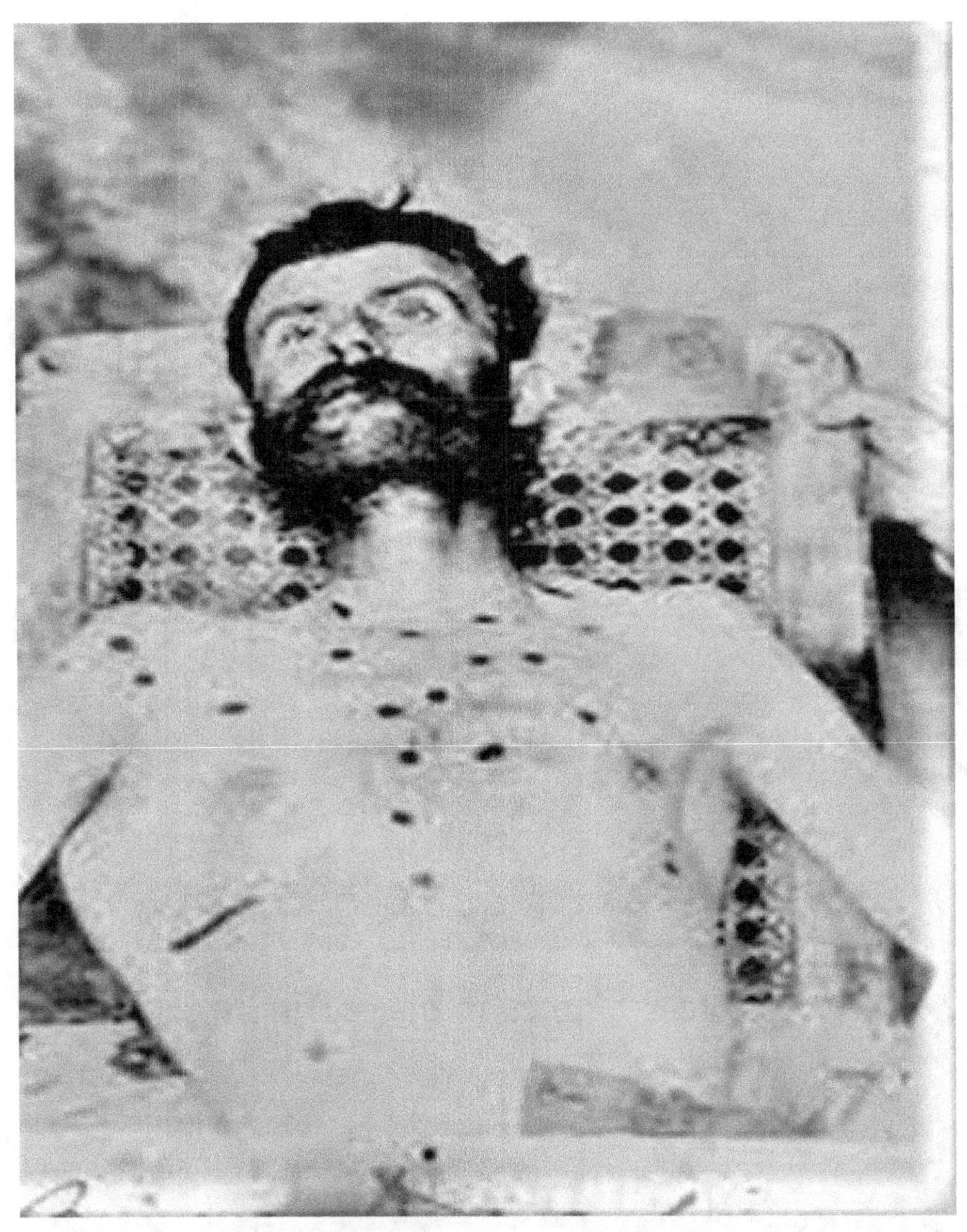

Outlaw Bill Doolin with bullet holes.

Jesse James in his coffin.

Four dead members of the Dalton Gang.

NOW, THE ALWAYS POPULAR, WTF'S!

Man claims this is the body of President Lincoln's assassin John Wilkes Booth. Who knows? Does it qualify as a WTF?

M16307

The Russian East Asiatic S.S. Co.   Radio-Telegram.

S.S. "Birma".

N Words.	Origin.Station.	Time handed in.	Via.	Remarks.
to	Titanic	about 1-40 a.m.		

c/o   SOS SOS CQD cqd - MGY

We are sinking fast passengers being put into boats
                                                    MGY

A Russian boat received the Titanic's SOS.

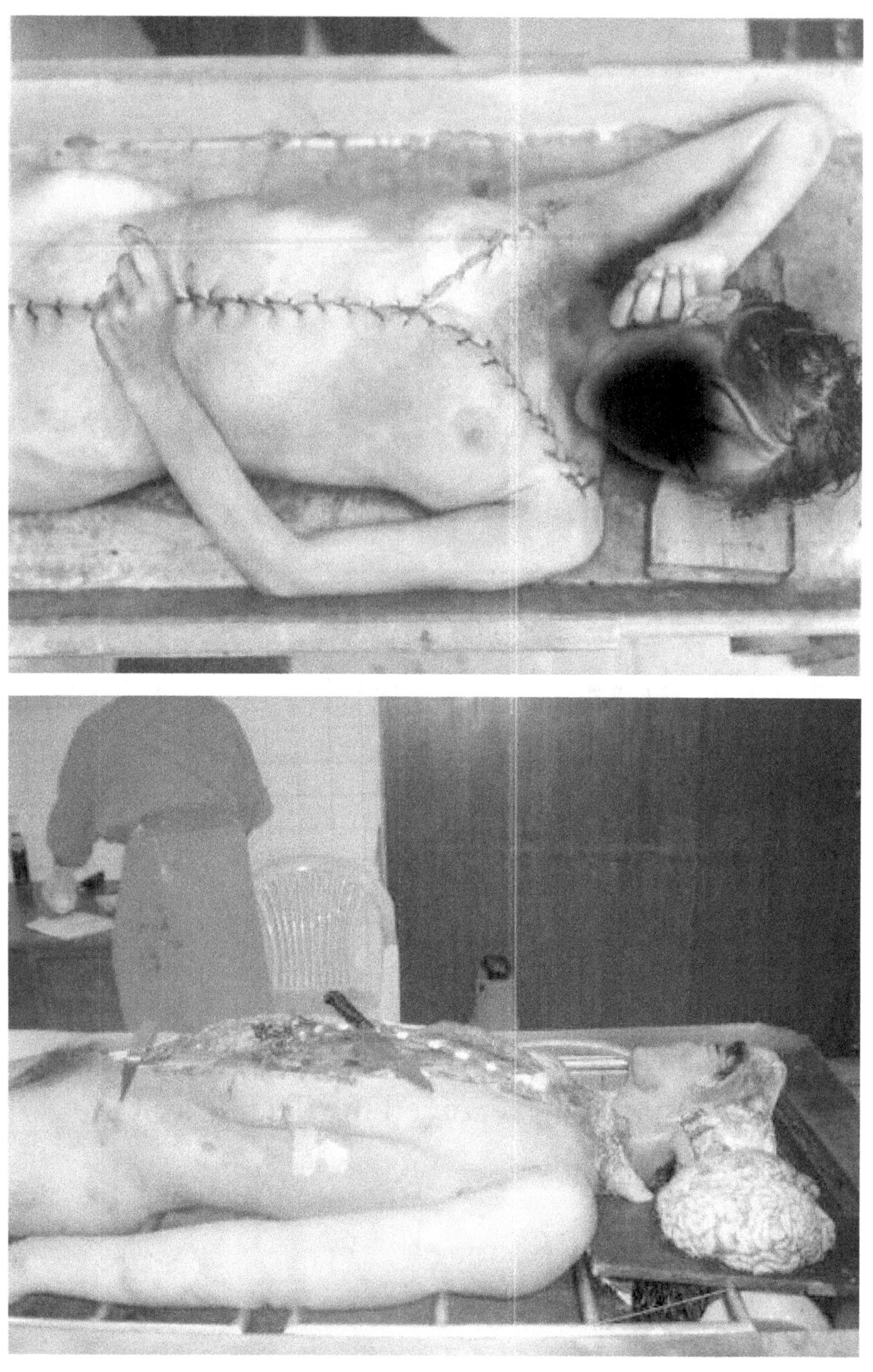

Autopsies. Lower with brain removed

Actor Bob Crane of the T.V. series Hogan's Hero's 1969.

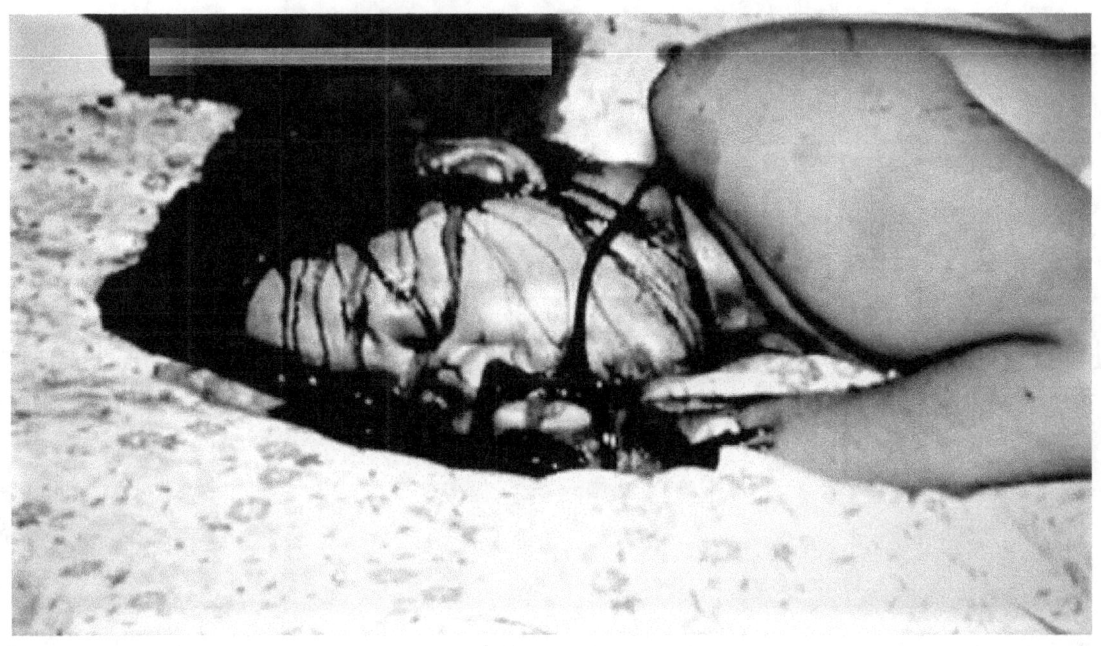

Bob Crane was murdered in bed.

25 Sept. 1888

Dear Boss

I keep on hearing the police have caught me but they wont fix me just yet. I have laughed when they look so clever and talk about being on the right track. That joke about Leather Apron gave me real fits. I am down on whores and I shant quit ripping them till I do get buckled. Grand work the last job was. I gave the lady no time to squeal. How can they catch me now. I love my work and want to start again. You will soon hear of me with my funny little games. I saved some of the proper red stuff in a ginger beer bottle over the last job to write with but it went thick like glue and I cant use it. Red ink is fit enough I hope ha. ha. The next job I do I shall clip the ladys ears off and send to the police officers just for jolly wouldn't you. Keep this letter back till I do a bit more work then give it out straight. My knife's so nice and sharp I want to get to work right away if I get a chance. Good luck.

yours truly
Jack the Ripper

Dont mind me giving the trade name

Letter from Jack the Ripper. An 18th century serial killer in England.

For decades, the government has claimed UFOs from another planet did not exist.

Yet, these two recent images from Navy fighters may prove otherwise.

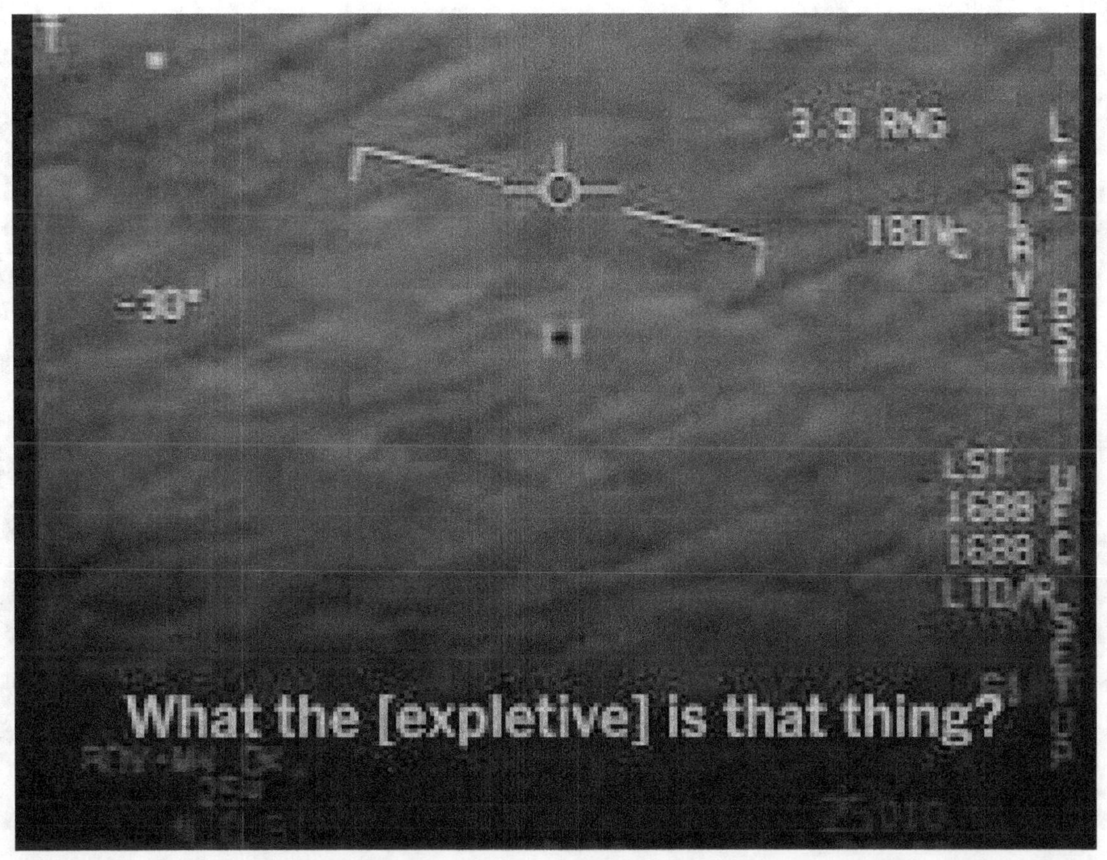

The Navy pilots were chasing this unknown flying object. It's the dark object in the center of the image with a white vertical line on each side.

WTF Navy?

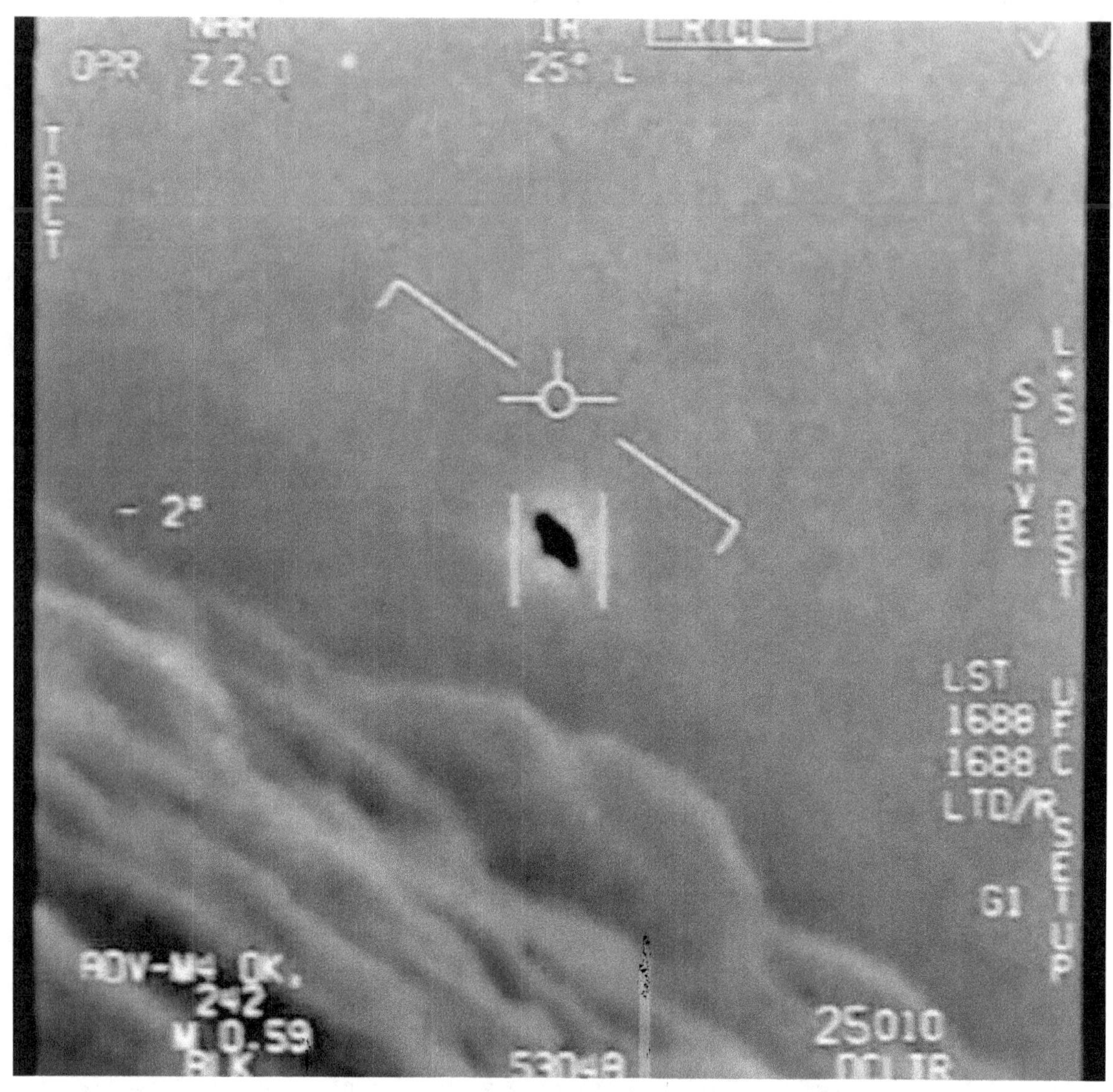

Another Navy WTF?

The pilots chasing this object had/have no idea what it was. It vanished at a high rate of speed.

For decades, hundreds, if not thousands of encounters of this nature have been reported by military and commercial pilots.

A tough life.

Chinese foot binding.

The thin man.

Muscle wasting, also known as muscle atrophy, is a loss of muscle tissue caused by decreased mobility or an underlying disease. Many neuromuscular and chronic inflammatory diseases are closely associated with muscle weakness, skeletal muscle atrophy, and muscle fatigue. Depending on the underlying cause, muscle atrophy can be partial or complete wasting away of muscles.

Emile Marie Bouchard had a14-inch waist.

An unfiltered cigarette! Outrageous!

Creepy dummy.

WTF?

Killing rats during Bubonic Plague.

Unwrapping a mummy.

WTF?

WTF?

WTF?

WTF?

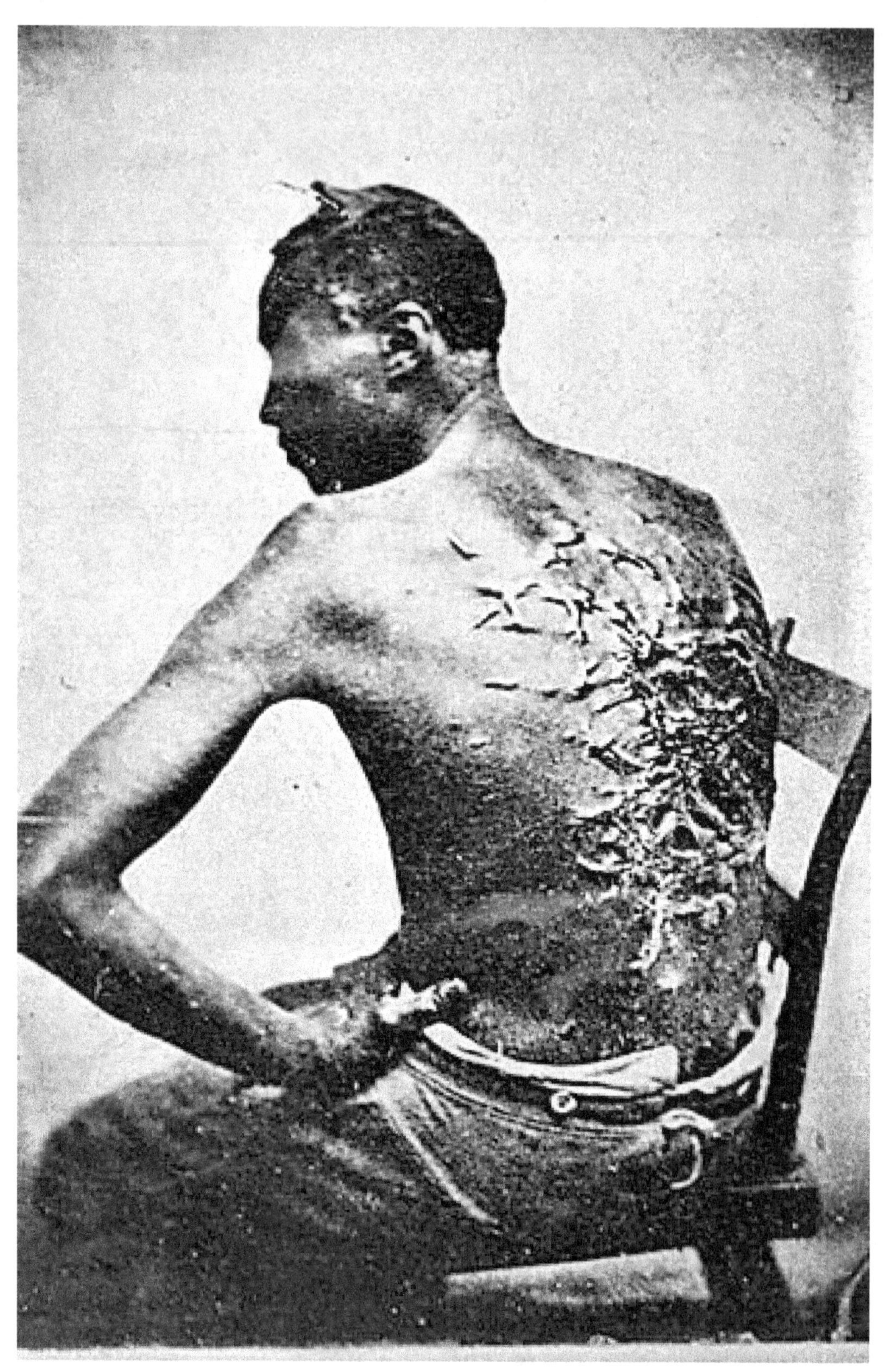

A whipped slave. Despicable.

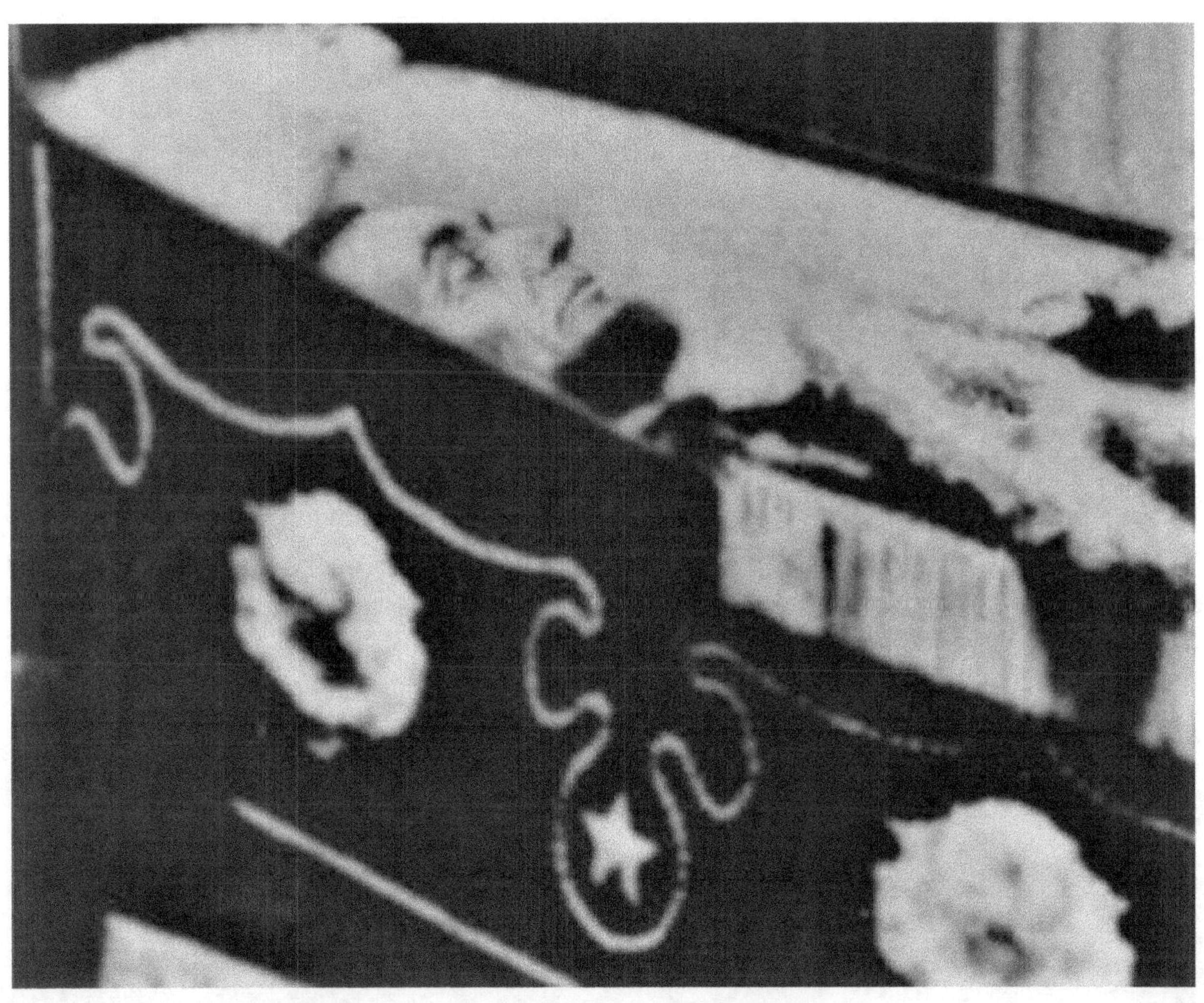

President Abraham Lincoln in a coffin.

St. Ubes.

London, June 28. Friday laſt the Vice-Chancellor of Cambridge in the Names of the Univerſity, the King, Prince, and Princeſs, and other Benefaċtors, laid the four firſt Stones, for the Foundation of a new Theatre.

A new engraven Stone is laid in Weſtminſter Abbey, over the burial Place of Thomas Par, born at Salop in 1483, and burying in 1635, and aged 152 Years, after having liv'd in ten Kings Reigns, viz. Thoſe of Edward IV. Edw. V. Richard III. King Henry VII. King Henry VIII. Edward VI. Queen Mary, Queen Elizabeth, King James, and King Charles.   Abun-

From the Newcastle Weekly Courant July 2, 1722.
Man lived 152 years.

Really?

Does it qualify as a WTF?

The list of names in the report of those   l living,
who had some role in the various activities, i long. The
names picked out in the review of the draft are below:

(1) James O'Connell
(2) Robert Maheu
(3) John Roselli
(4) Santos Trafficante
(5) (FNU) Maceo
(6) Tony Varona
(7) Juan Orta
(8) J. C. King
(9) William Harvey
(10) Samuel Halpern
(11) Bronson Tweedy
(12) Sidney Gottlieb
(13) ████████
(14) Edward Gunn
(15) (FNU) Gomez (otherwise unidentified in text)
(16) Henry Dearborn
(17) John Barfield
(18) ████████
(19) Alonzo Berry
(20) Colonel Wimert
(21) David Phillips
(22) Justin O'Donnell
(23) Glenn Fields
(24) Lou Conein
(25) John Richardson
(26) David R. Smith

This list omits persons not directly involved other than in the
line of command, from the level of Deputy Director up. Two division
chiefs are listed--J. C. King and Bronson Tweedy--and might, by reasc
of their seniority, be omitted from the list of those whose names
should be deleted. The list, otherwise, is a mix of Agency employees,
cooperating individuals, and agents. The comments below first treat
the question of Agency employees.

- 2 -

The official list of CIA assassins obtained
from Congressional records.

KING,

In view of your low grade, abnormal personal behavoir I
will not dignify your name with either a Mr. or a Reverend or
a Dr. And, your last name calls to mind only the type of
King such as King Henry the VIII and his countless acts of
adultery and immoral conduct lower than that of a beast.

King, look into your heart. You know you are a complete
fraud and a great liability to all of us Negroes. White
people in this country have enough frauds of their own but I
am sure they don't have one at this time that is any where near
your equal. You are no clergyman and you know it. I repeat you
are a colossal fraud and an evil, vicious one at that. You
could not believe in God and act as you do. Clearly you don't
believe in any personal morel principles.

King, like all frauds your end is approaching. You could
have been our greatest leader. You, even at an early age have
turned out to be not a leader but a dissolute, abnormal moral
imbecile. We will now have to depend on our older leaders like
Wilkins a man of character and thank God we have others like
him. But you are done. Your "honorary" degrees, your Nobel
Prize (what a grim farce) and other awards will not save you.
King, I repeat you are done.

No person can overcome facts, not even a fraud like yourself.
Lend your sexually psychotic ear to the enclosure. You will find
yourself and in all your dirt, filth, evil and moronic
talk exposed on the record for all time. I repeat - no person
can argue successfully against facts. You are finished. You will
find on the record for all time your filthy, dirty, evil
companions, male and females giving expression with you to your
hidious abnormalities. And some of them to pretend to be ministers
of the Gospel. Satan could not do more. What incredible evilness.
It is all there on the record, your sexual orgies. Listen to
yourself you filthy, abnormal animal. You are on the record. You
have been on the record - all your adulterous acts, your sexual
orgies extending far into the past. This one is but a tiny sample.
You will understand this. Yes, from your various evil playmates
on the east coast to Dolores Evans and others on the west coast
and outside the country you are on the record. King you are done.

The American public, the church organizations that have been
helping - Prostestant, Catholic and Jews will know you for what
you are - an evil, abnormal beast. So will others who have backed
you. You are done.

King, there is only one thing left for you to do. You know
what it is. You have just 34 days in which to do (this exact
number has been selected for a specific reason, it has definite
practical significant. You are done. There is but one way out for
you. You better take it before your filthy, abnormal fraudulent self
is bared to the nation.

Secret hate letter J. Edgar Hoover wrote to Martin Luther King.
This letter was found in Hoover's personal file after his death.

Statue of Liberty head on display Paris 1878.

Artificial legs 1890.

Princeton students after an 1893 snowball fight.

The Hindenburg airship disaster
May 6, 1937, at Manchester, New Jersey
36 killed. 62 survived.

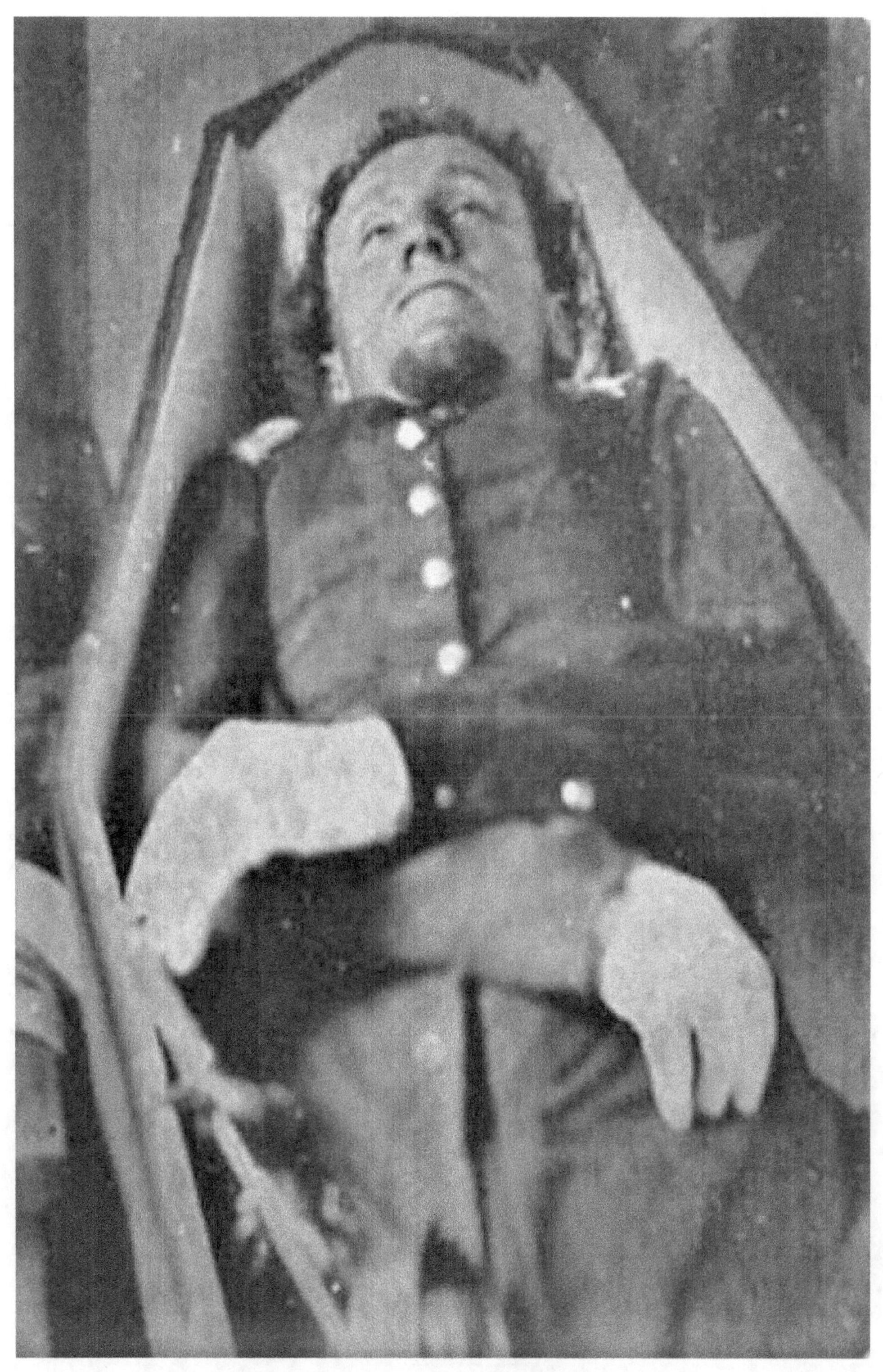

Civil War soldier in a coffin.

THE MUMMIES

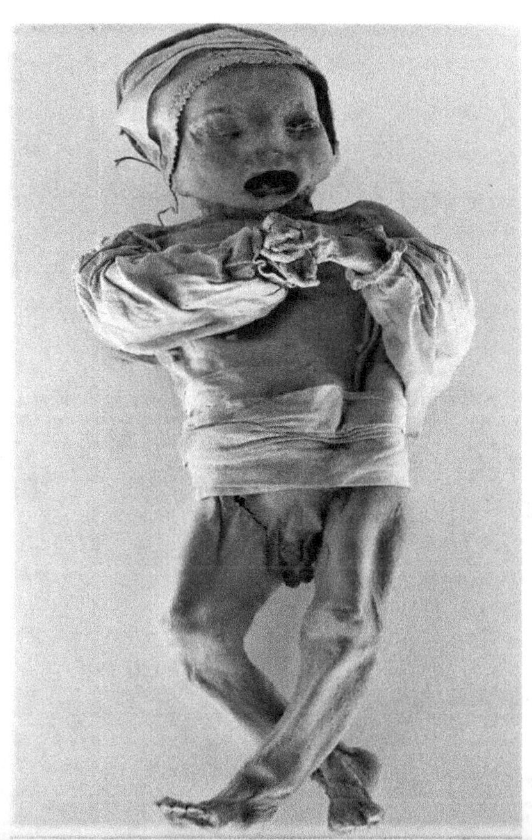

Mummies Guanajuato, Mexico.
Courtesy of The Mummy Museum.

Mummy of a woman.
Courtesy of The Mummy Museum
Guanajuato, Mexico.

Children mummies.
Courtesy of The Mummy Museum
Guanajuato, Mexico.

EGYPTIAN MUMMIES

King Tutankhamun
Howard Carter unearthed King Tuts tomb in 1922.

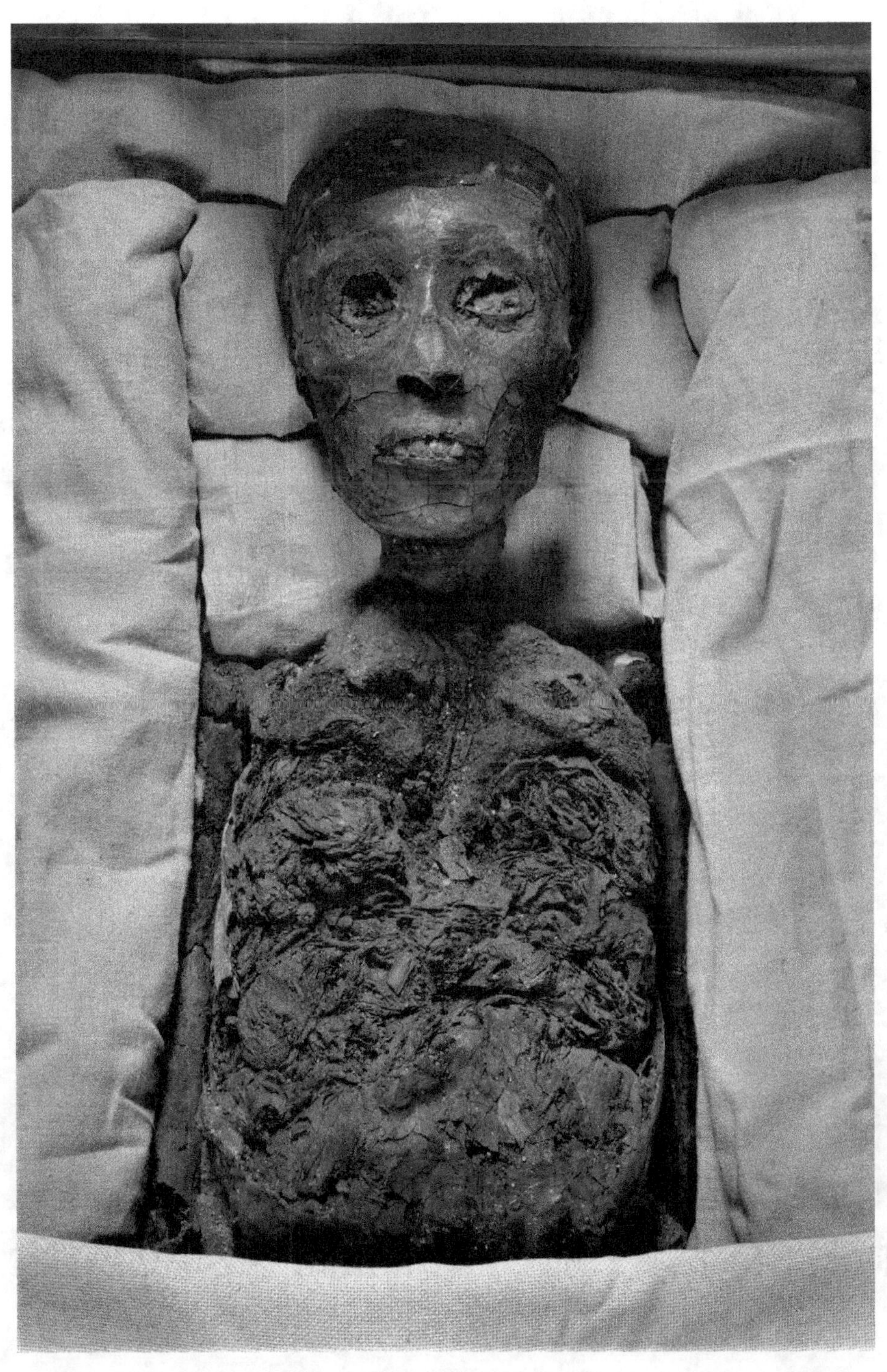

King Tutankhamun. He ruled Egypt from 1321-1325 B.C.

King Seti 1. He ruled Egypt from 1324-1279 B.C.

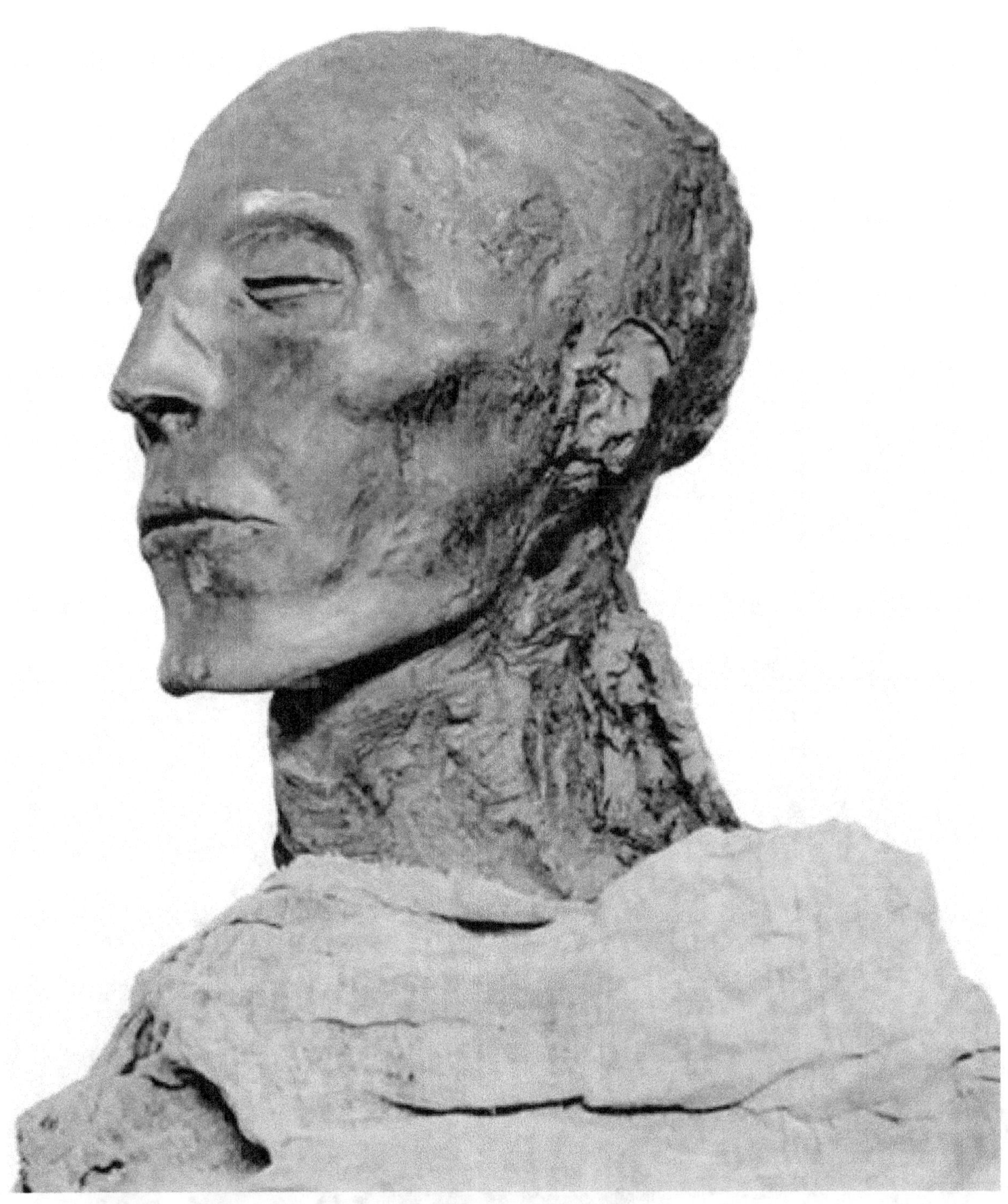

Seti 1

The Egyptians mummified a variety of animals.

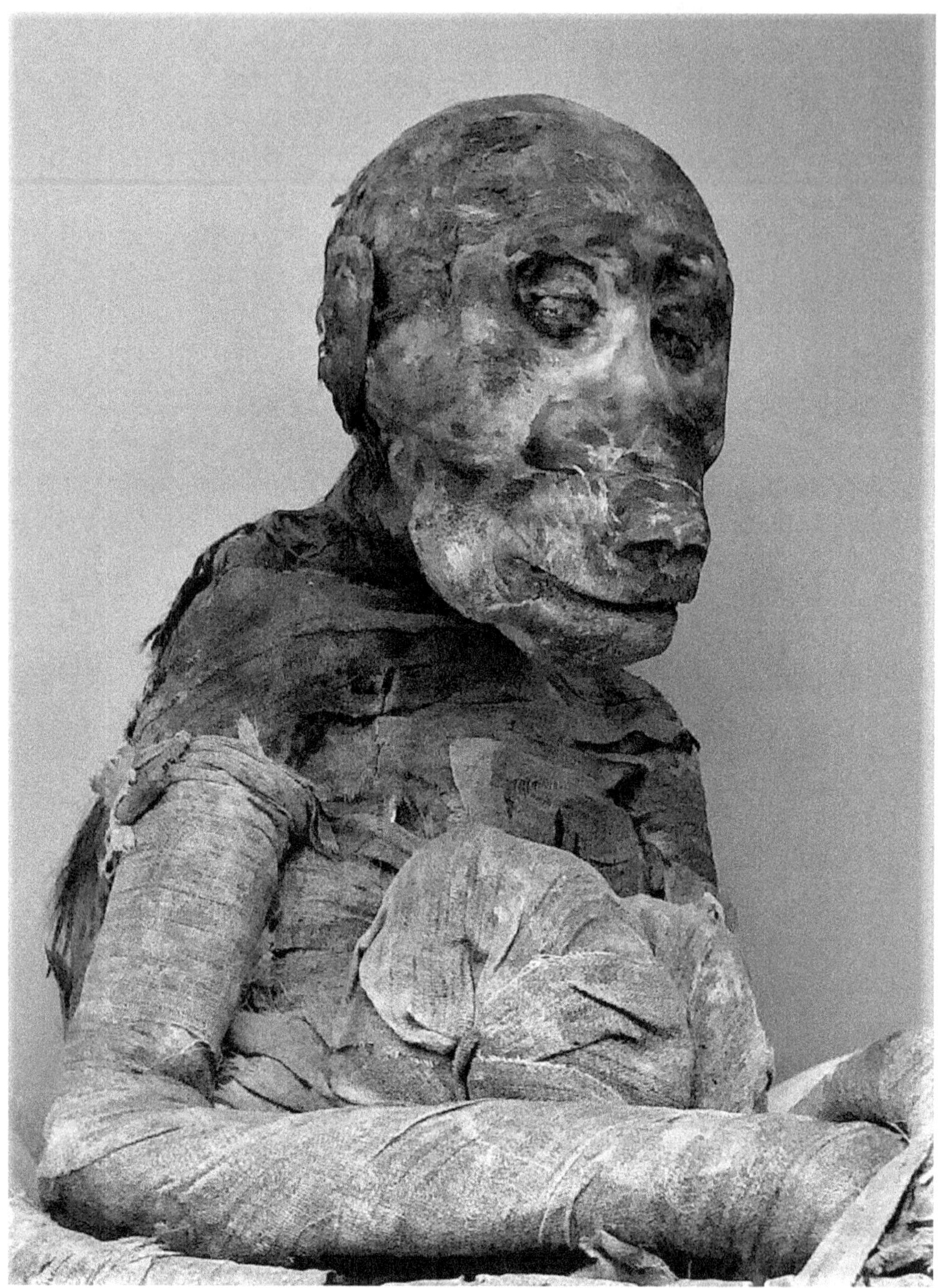

Mummified baboon.

Mummified falcon.

AMERICAN LYNCHINGS

WHITE MOBS LYNCHED THOUSANDS OF AFRICAN AMERICANS DURING THE 18TH AND 19TH CENTURIES. THE EXACT NUMBER WILL NEVER BE KNOWN.

INTERESTINGLY, DURING THAT TIME, AFRICAN AMERICAN MOBS ALSO LYNCHED AFRICAN AMERICANS FOR ALLEGEDLY THE SAME REASONS AS THE WHITE MOBS.

MOBS MUST NEVER DISPENSE JUSTICE. EVERYONE IS ENTITLED TO A FAIR TRIAL.

Crowd watches after lynching an African American and then burning the body.

The lynching of an African American woman.

Four African American's lynched. Today, no one knows why.

THE SLAUGHTER OF NATIVE AMERICANS BY THE U.S. GOVERNMENT.

Chief Bigfoot's frozen body at the Wounded Knee Massacre.

On December 29, 1890, more than 200 Sioux men, women, and children were massacred by U.S. troops in what has been called the Battle of Wounded Knee.

Burying the dead at Wounded Knee.

Bodies at Wounded Knee.

Bodies at Wounded Knee.

Collecting Indian bodies for burial at Wounded Knee.

Bodies of Crow Indians killed and scalped by Sioux Indians.

Indian tribes did war with other tribes.

White man killed by Indians.

VICTORIAN ERA DEATH PHOTOGRAPHY

At the time, it was considered normal to have a dead family member propped up or posed with the remaining family members for a final photograph. The dead were posed in lifelike positions, and sometimes eyes were painted on closed eyelids to make them appear living. Today, the practice is considered grotesque.

Also, it was not uncommon for couples to have many children during the Victorian era since numerous kids died before age 5.

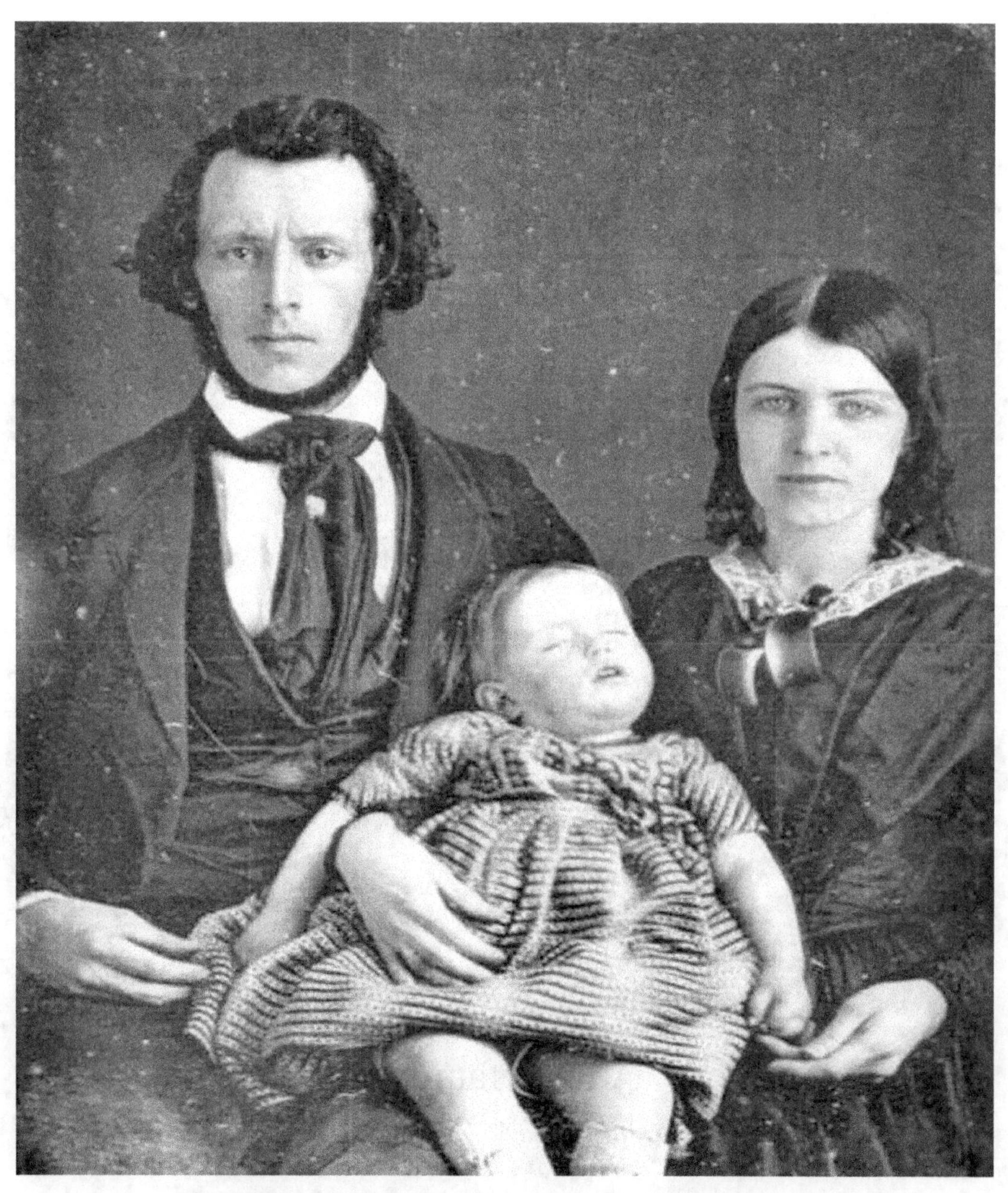

Parents photographed with dead child.

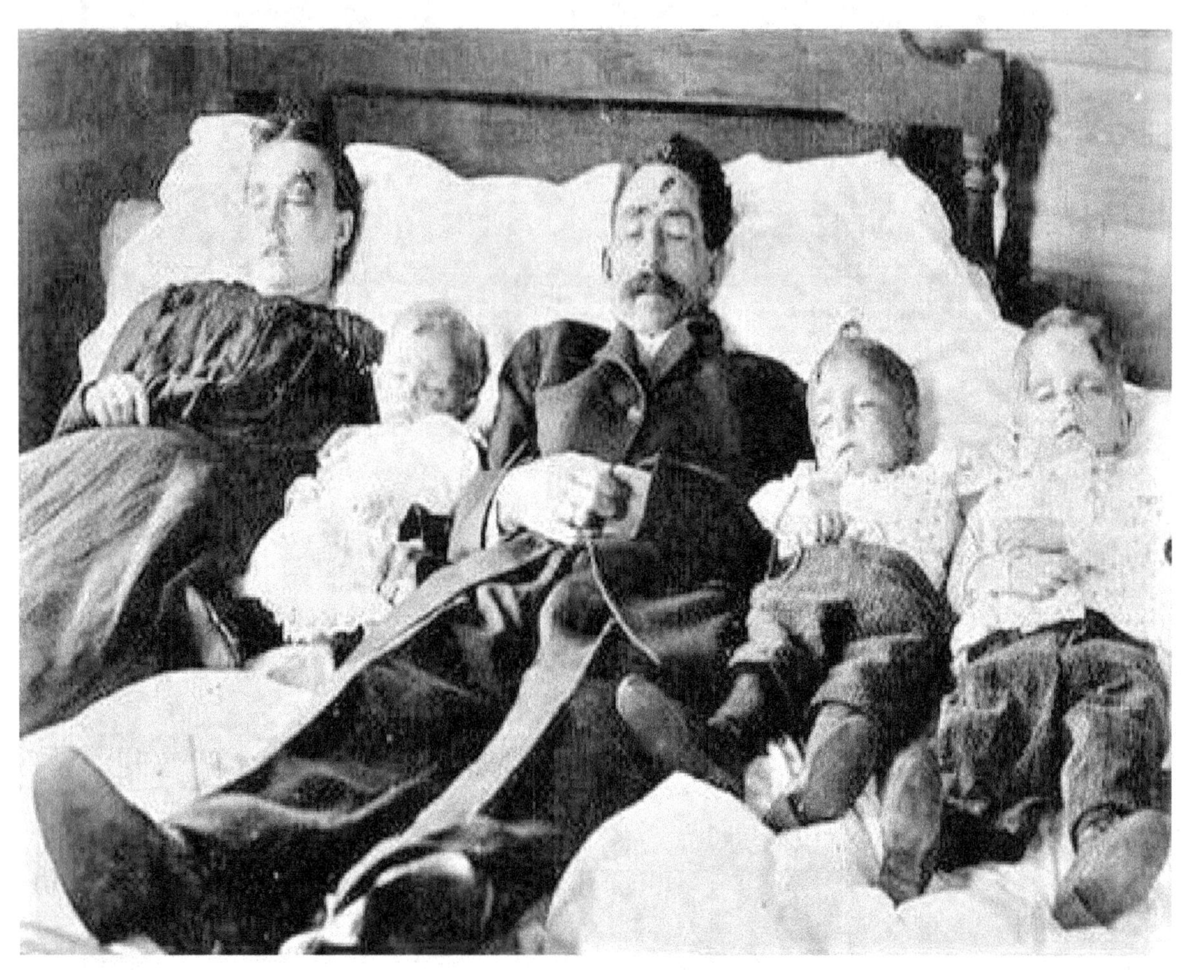

A dead family.

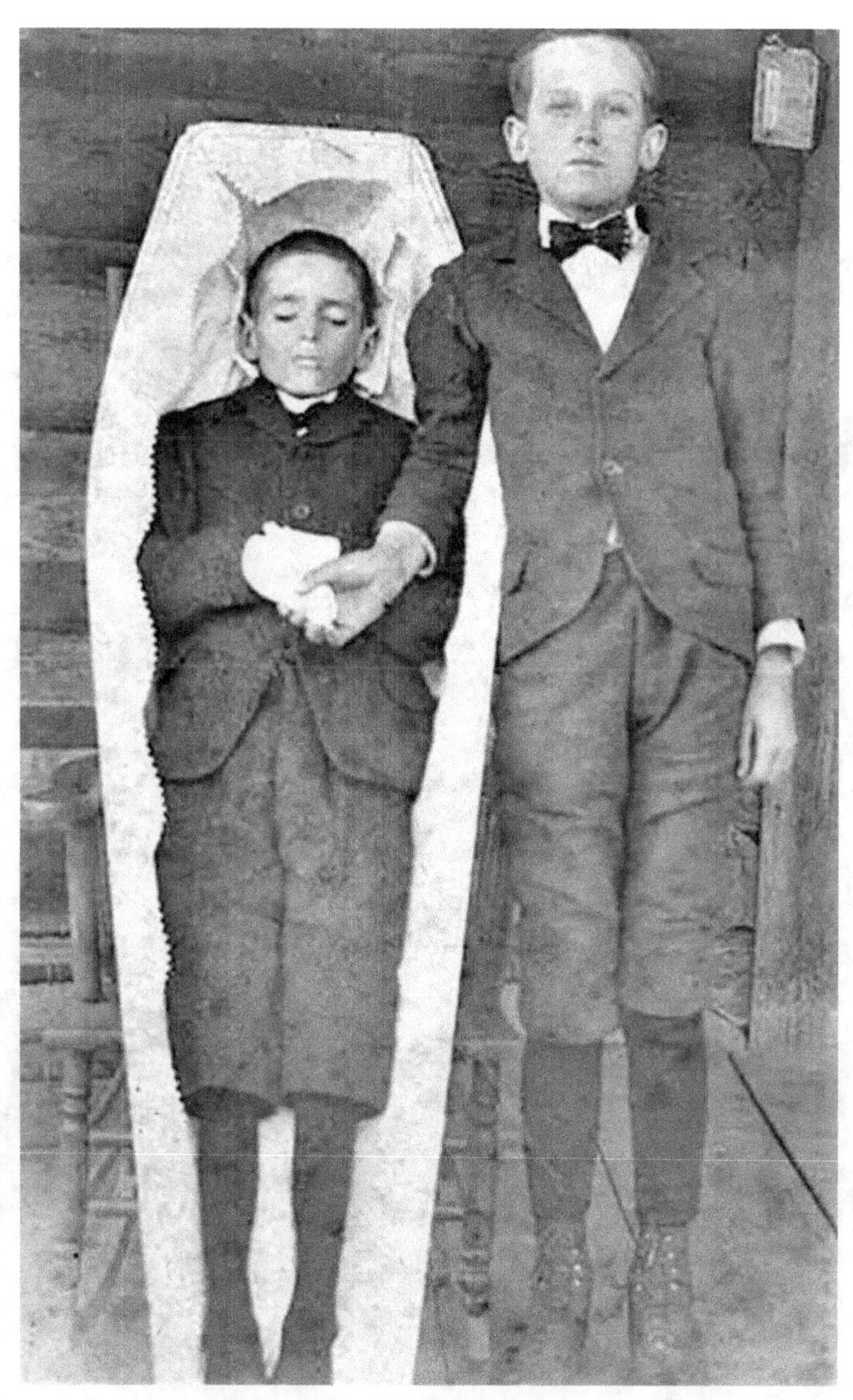

Holding his dead brother's hand.

Photographing dead man in a chair.

Is she living or dead?

The little girl on the left is dead. Her body was propped up for a final family photograph.

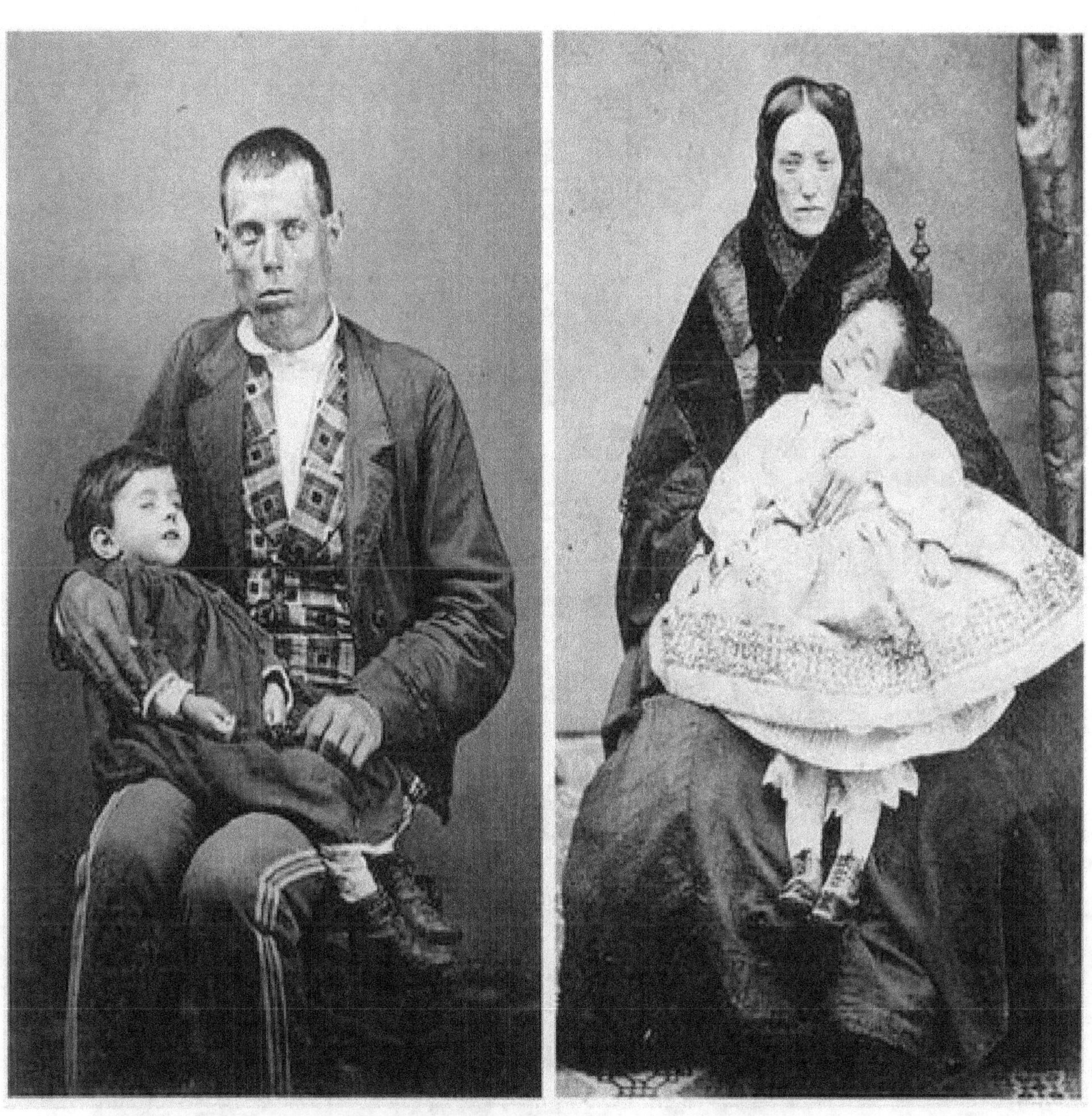

Posing with their dead children.

Sisters posing with their dead mother.

Posing with a dead relative. The woman at the lower right is
dead.

Parents pose with their dead daughter.

Note the parents are blurred, and the daughter's image is sharp. Long camera exposures were required at the time, resulting in the living slightly moving and blurring the picture, while the dead remained motionless, resulting in a sharp image.

A father posing with his dead child.

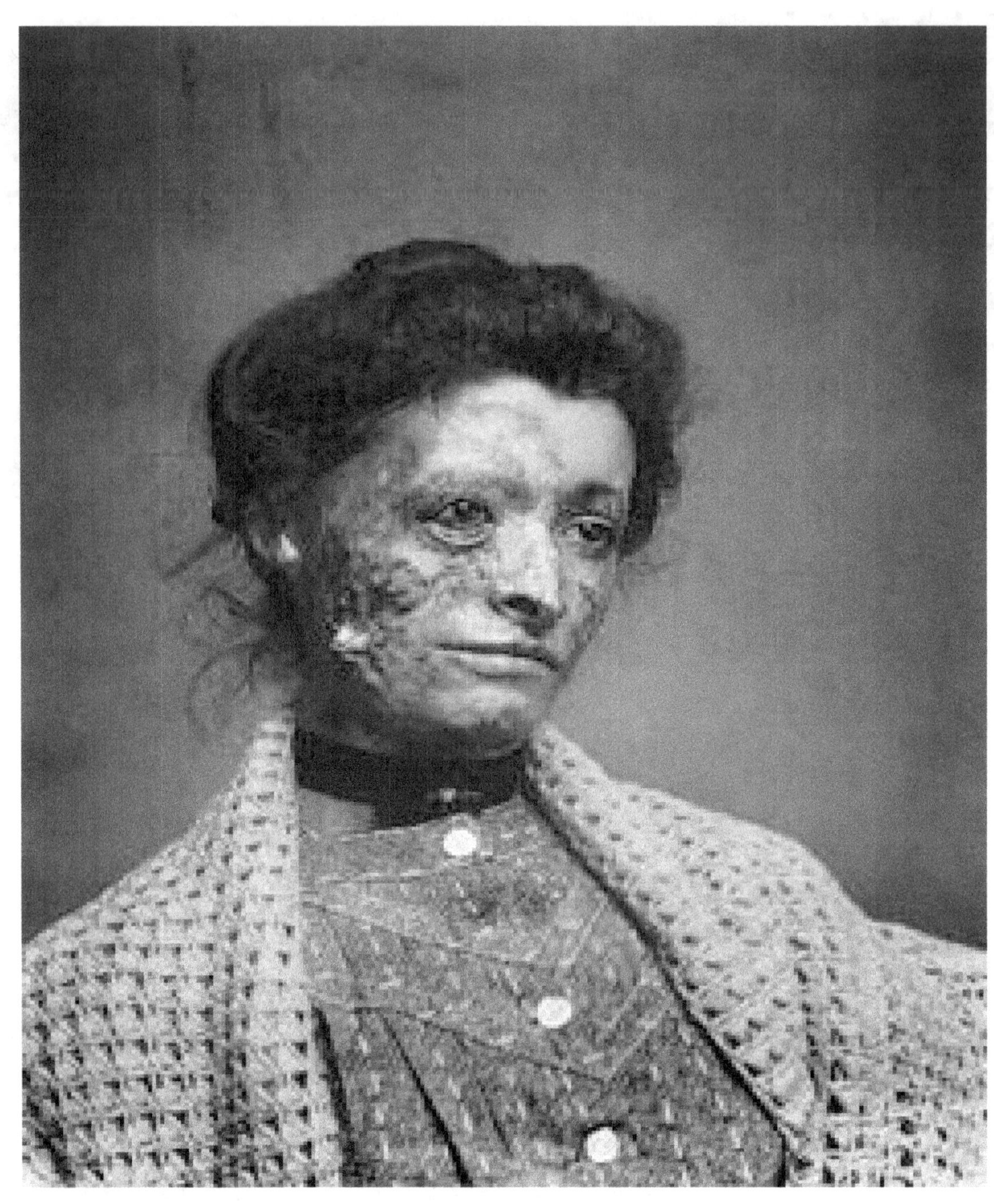

Her eyes are propped open.

Child holding her dead sister's hand. The deceased is on the left.

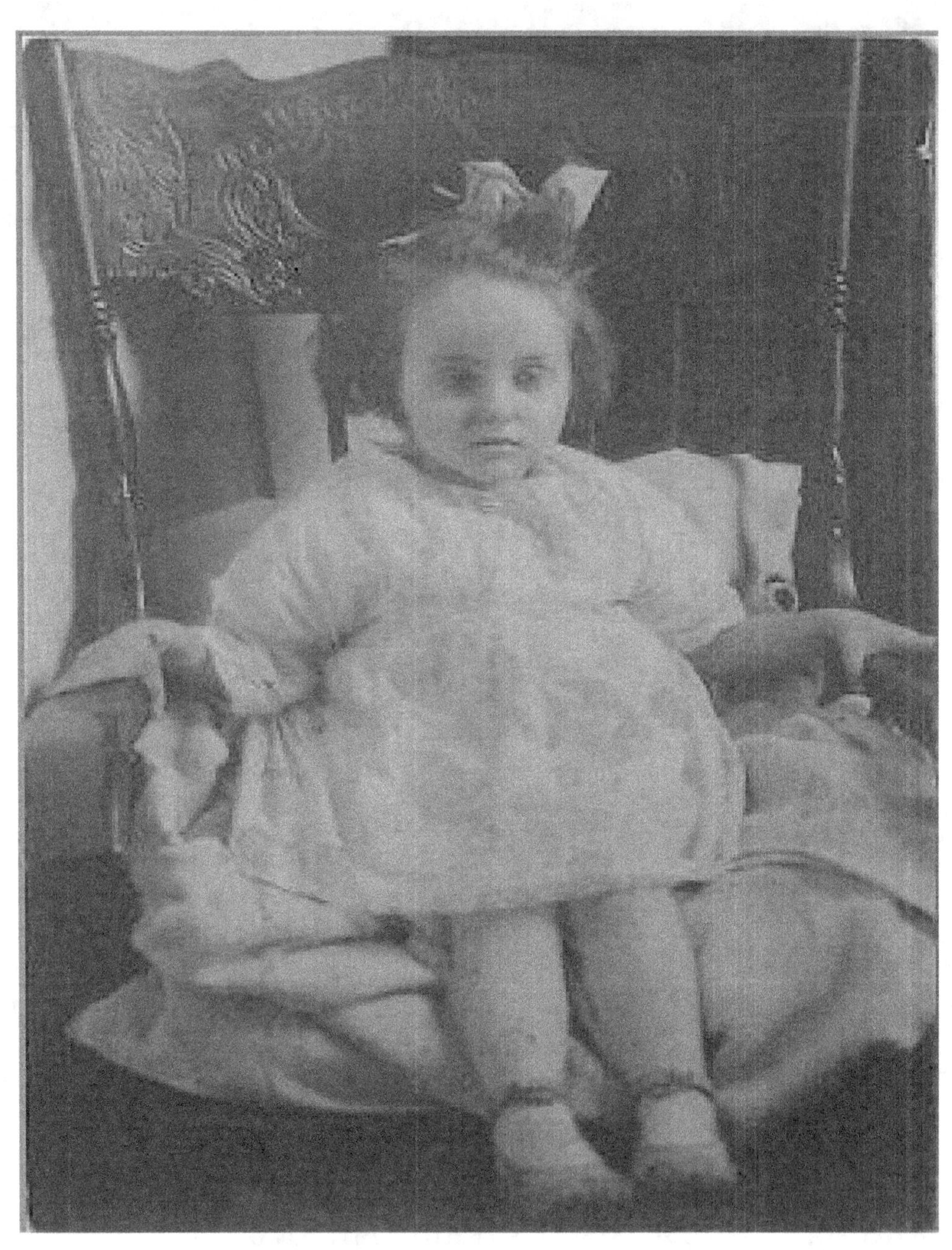

Dead child posed in rocking chair.

Family posing with dead twins.

Creepy!

HUMAN ODDITIES

During the 1800s, many people suffering from various abnormalities were on display in the *Freak Shows* of a circus or carnival. Congenital disabilities and illnesses are not the faults of the people suffering from the disorders.

Elephantiasis is the result of a parasitic infection caused by three specific kinds of roundworms. The long, threadlike worms block the body's lymphatic system— a network of channels, lymph nodes, and organs that helps maintain proper fluid levels in the body by draining lymph from tissues into the bloodstream. This block age causes fluids to collect in the tissues, leading to significant swelling, called "lymphedema." Blood-sucking insects, primarily mosquitoes, cause the infection.

Elephantiasis

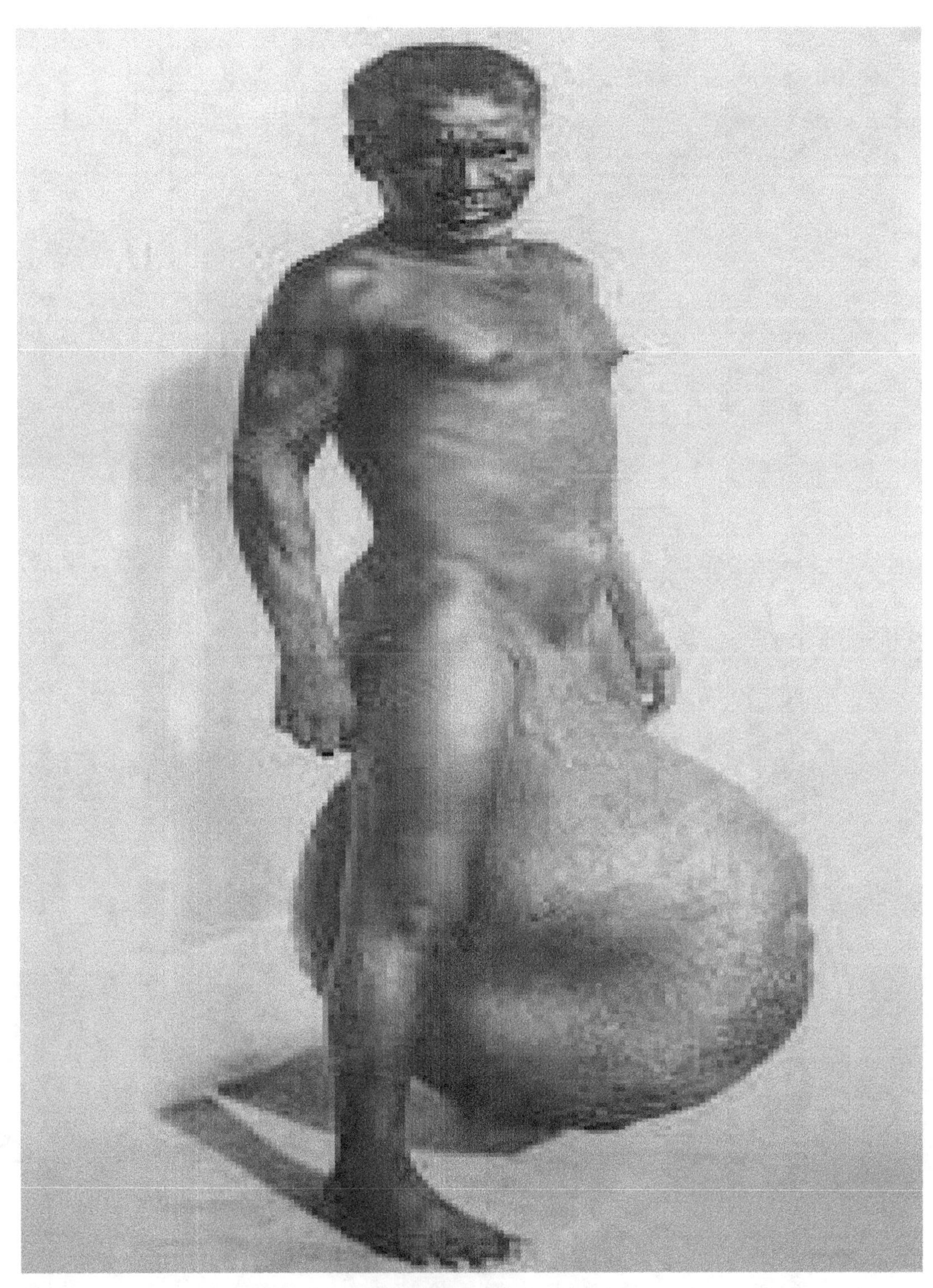

Scrotal Elephantiasis

Elephantiasis 1614

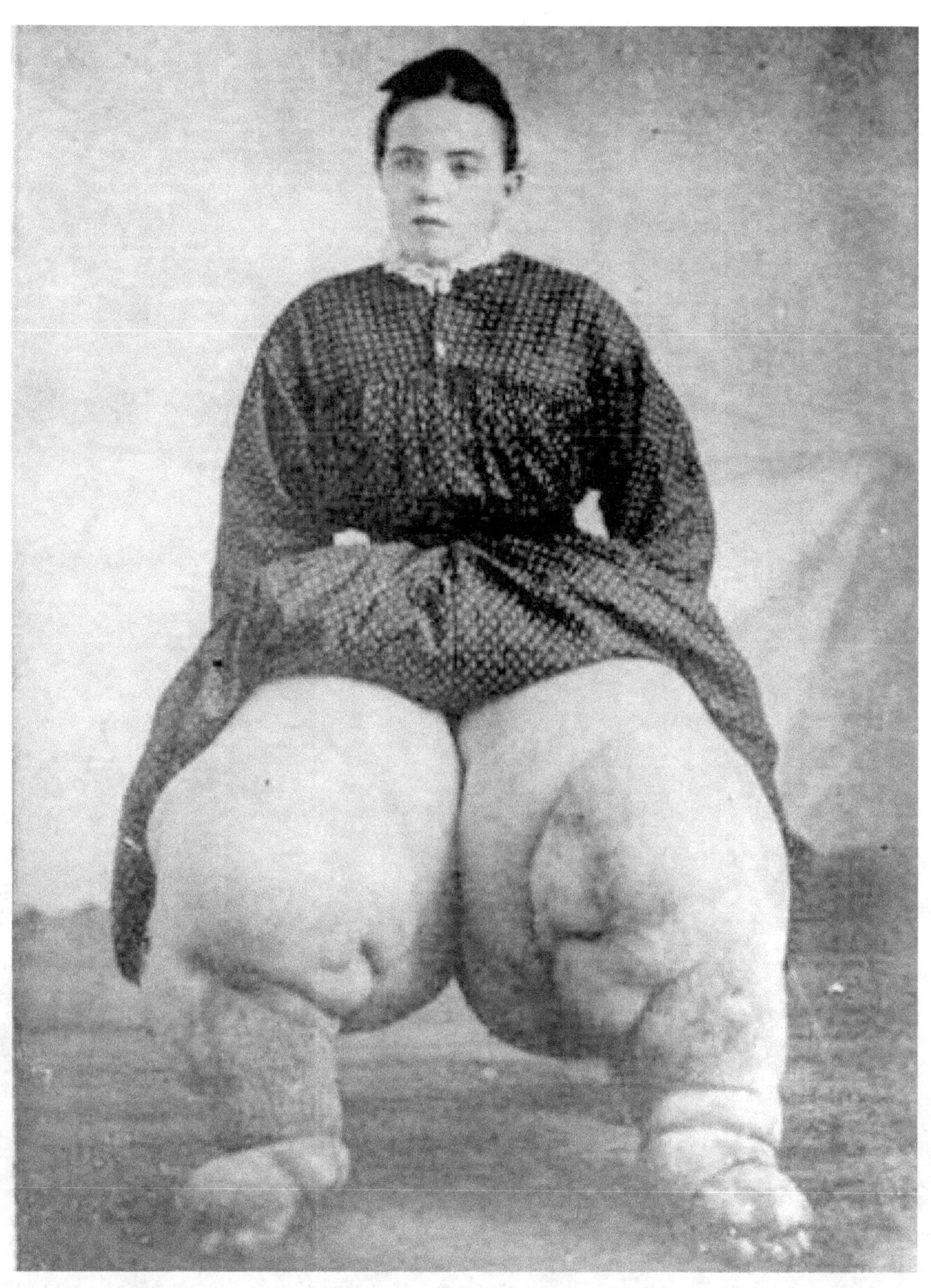

Elephantiasis

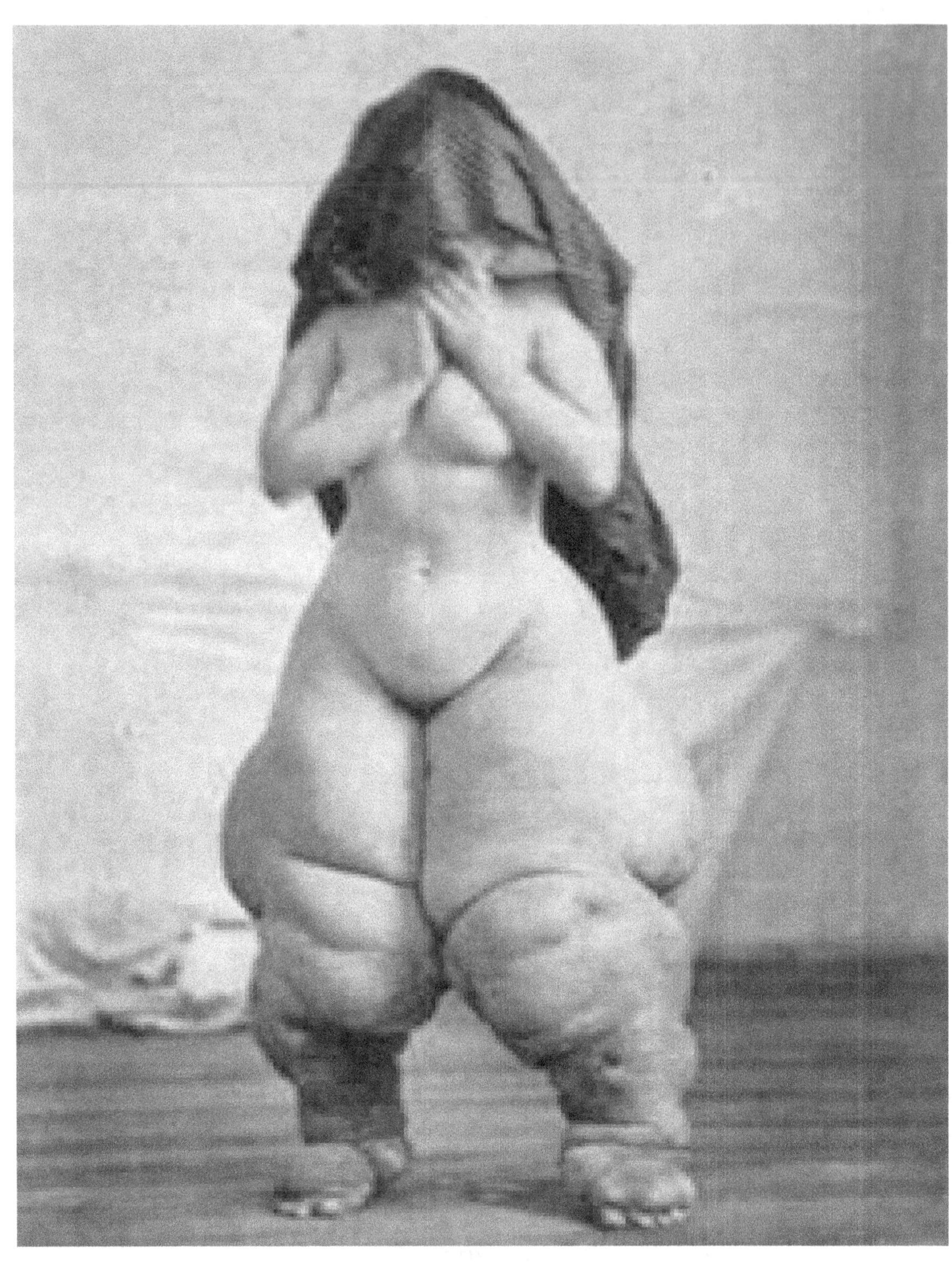

Elephantiasis

From the Victorian Era

Elephant Man Joseph Merritt.

For years it was thought Joseph suffered from a severe case of neurofibromatosis. Later it is believed his deformities were most likely the result of a rare disease known as Proteus Syndrome.

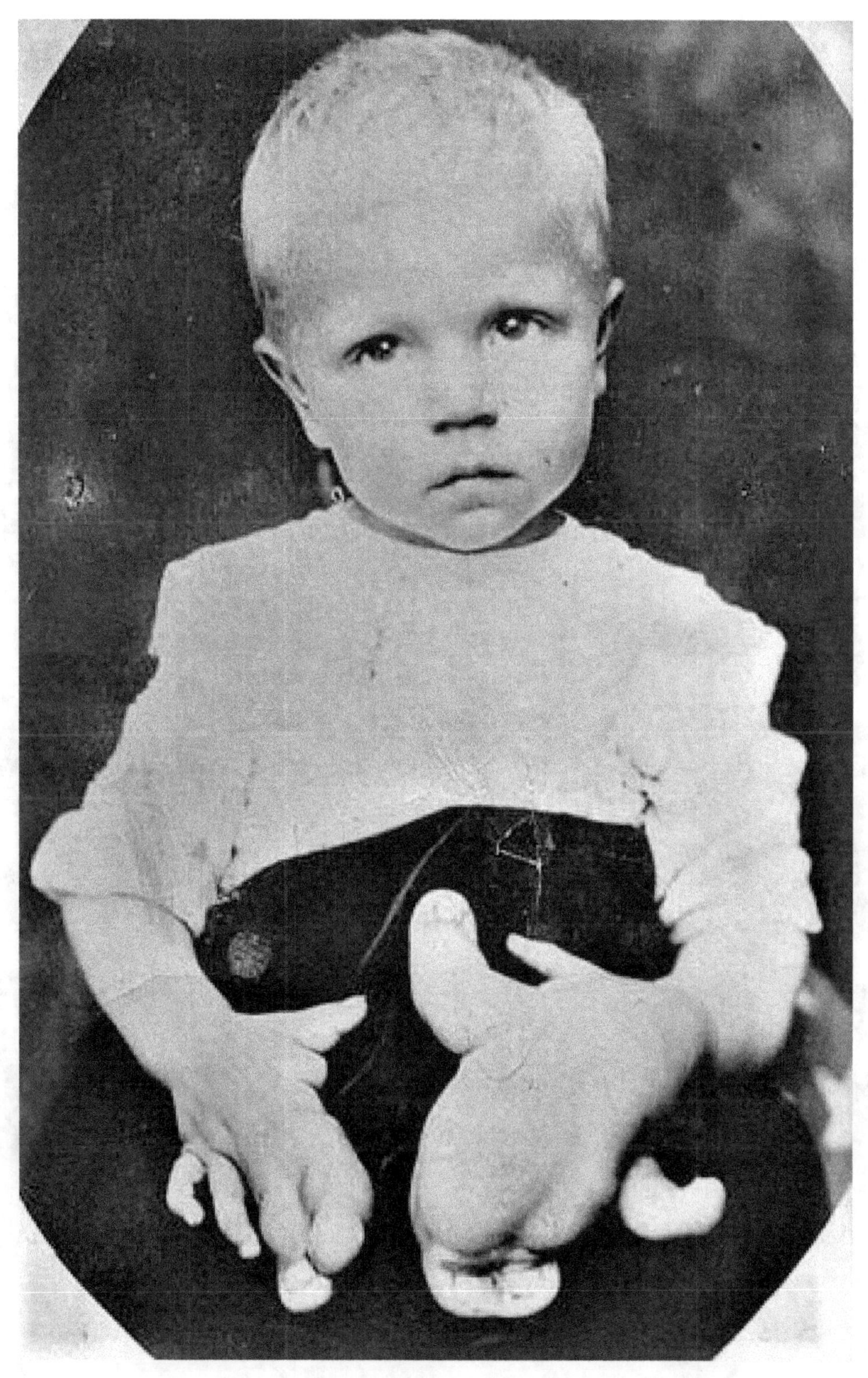

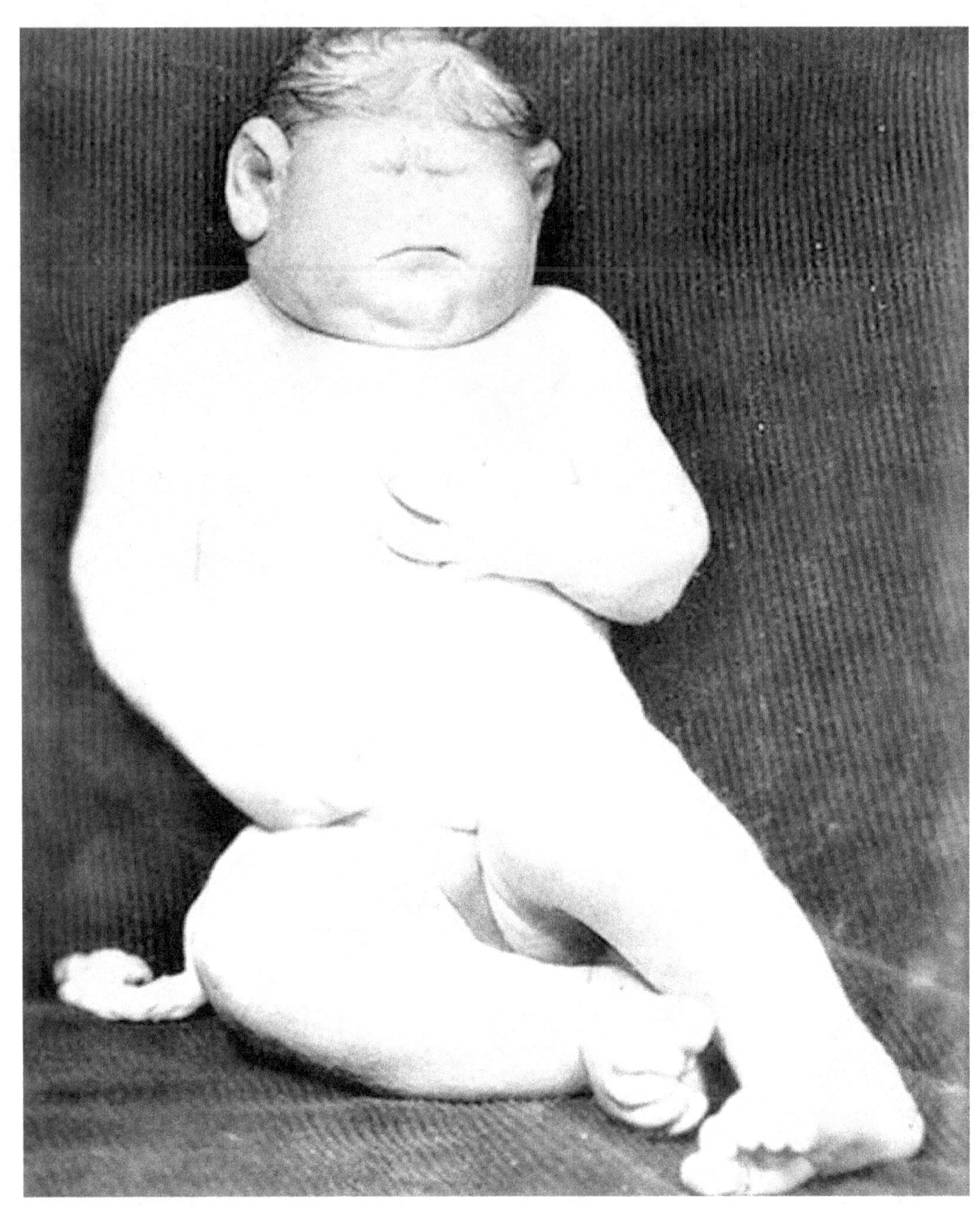

Congenital disability. The child did not survive.

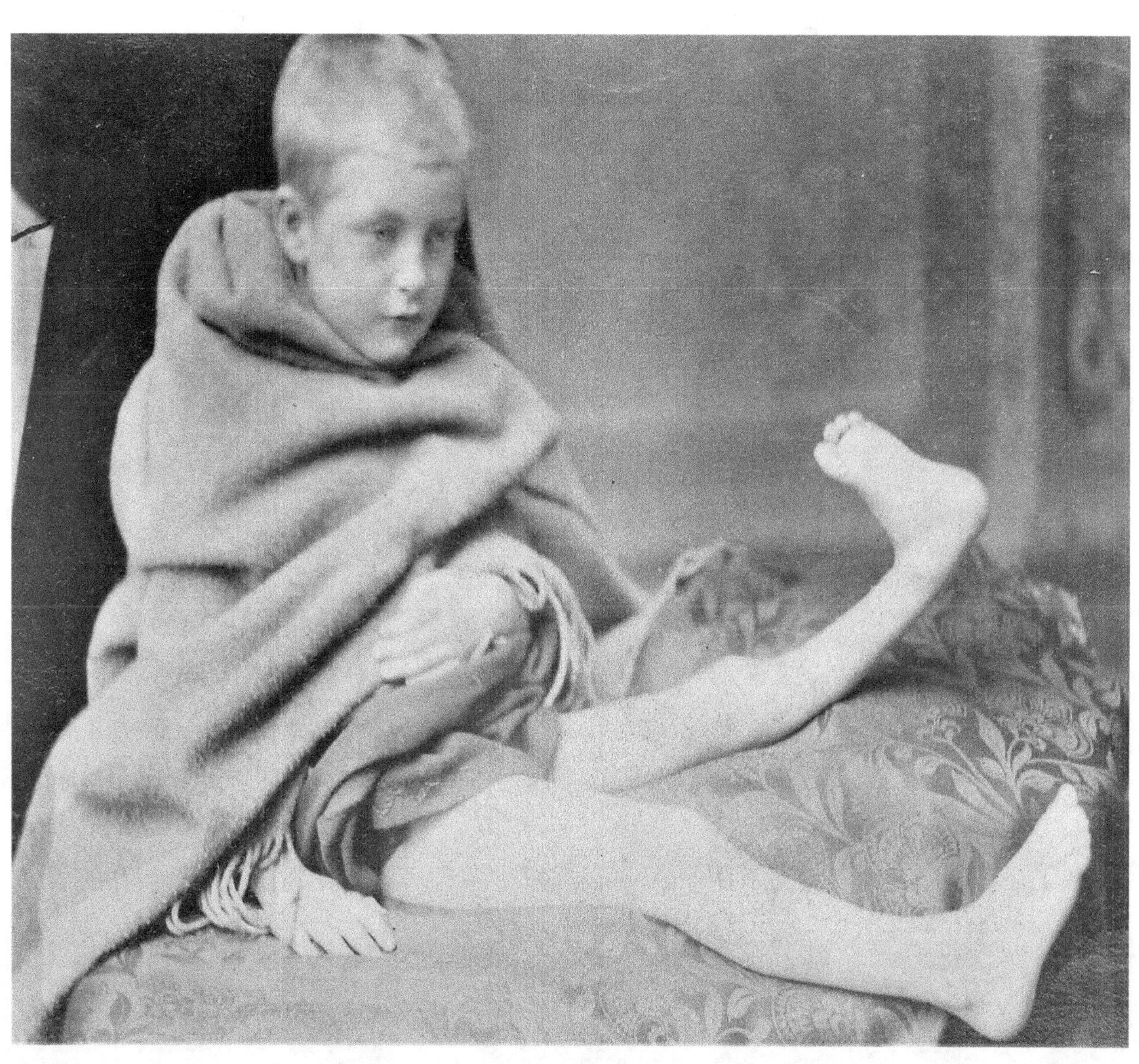

She was called the "Leopard Girl" and suffered from Vitiligo.

It is a long-term skin condition characterized by patches of the skin losing their pigment.

Ectrodactyly or "Lobster Hands"

Ectrodactyly is a congenital limb malformation, characterized by a deep median cleft of the hand and/or foot due to the absence of central rays. Affected individuals may be recognized by a lobster-claw deformity of their limb extremities that causes severe functional disorders.

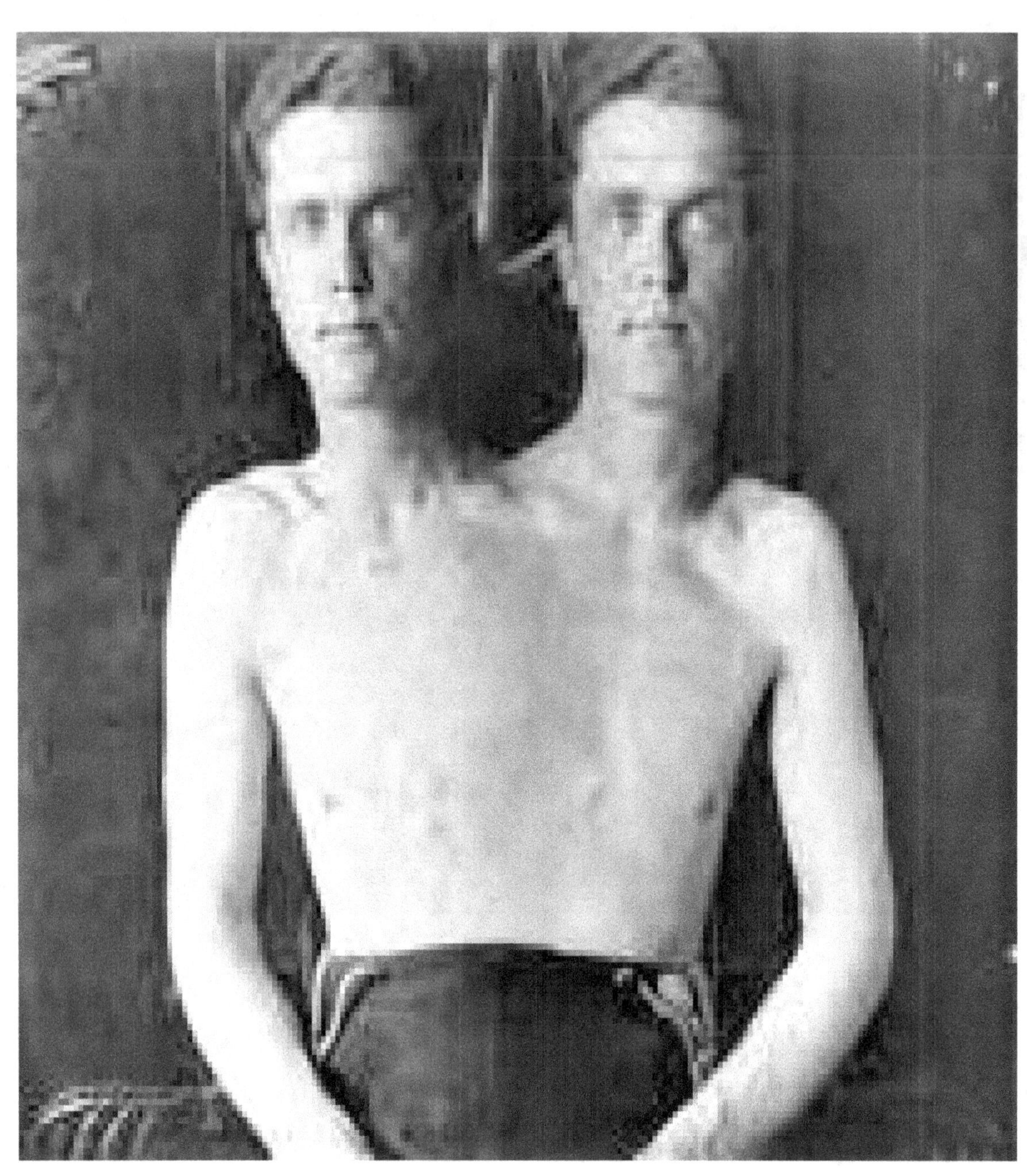

Conjoined twins.

The Colloredo Brothers illustration.

Conjoined twins.

Considered conjoined.

Considered conjoined.

Considered conjoined.

Thin and obese from a circus "Freak Show."

1656 AD, Barbara Vanbeck.

Case of Hypertrichosis.

Madame Colfullia the bearded lady 1850

Hypertrichosis.

Two cases of Hypertrichosis.

ILLUSTRATIONS OF MEDIEVAL TORTURE

THE IMAGES SPEAK FOR THEMSELVES.

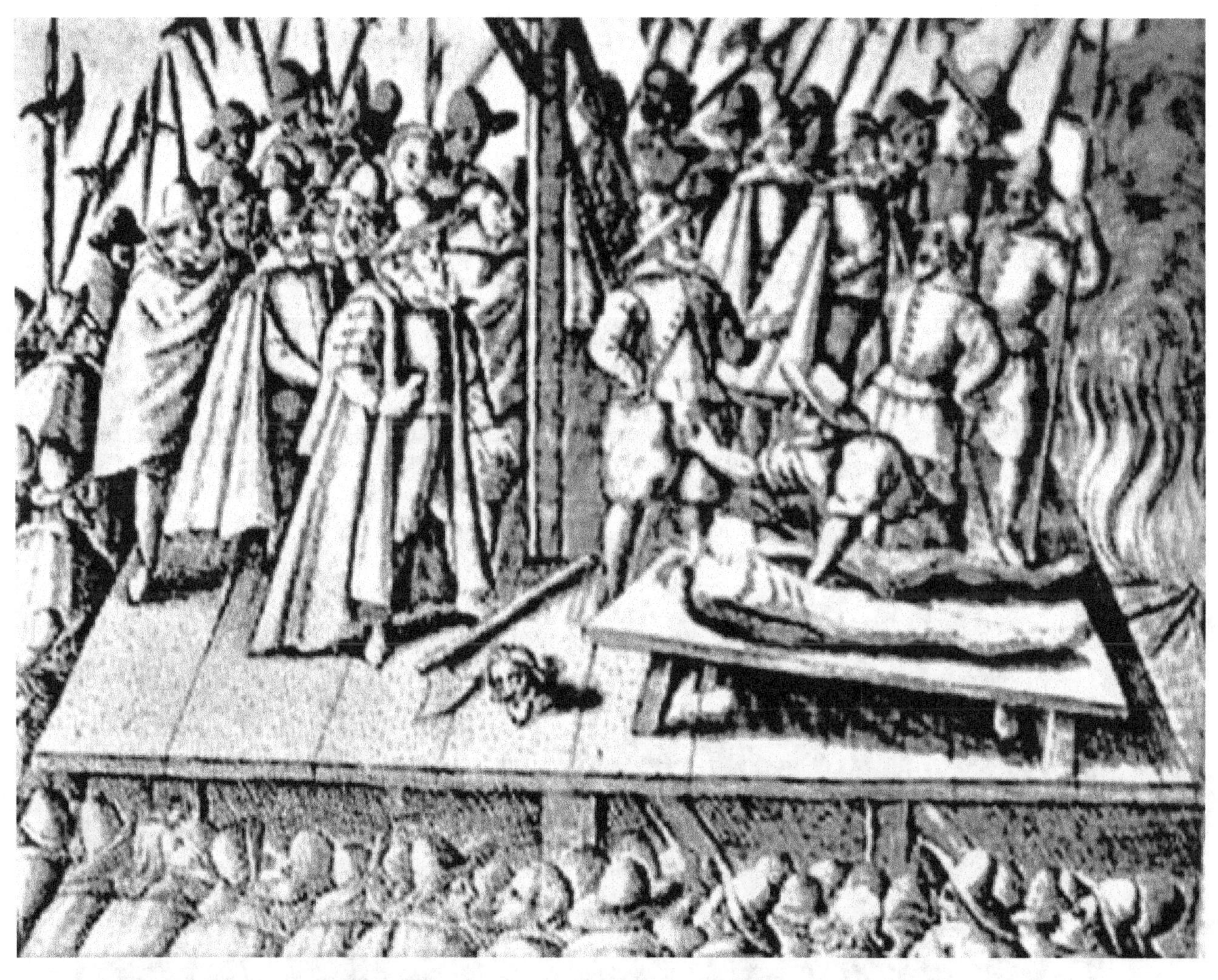

Beheading after torturing of Guy Fawkes.

In 1604 Fawkes and a small group of English Catholics, led
by Robert Catesby, planned to assassinate the Protestant King
James and replace him with his daughter. The conspiracy failed.

A
B
27

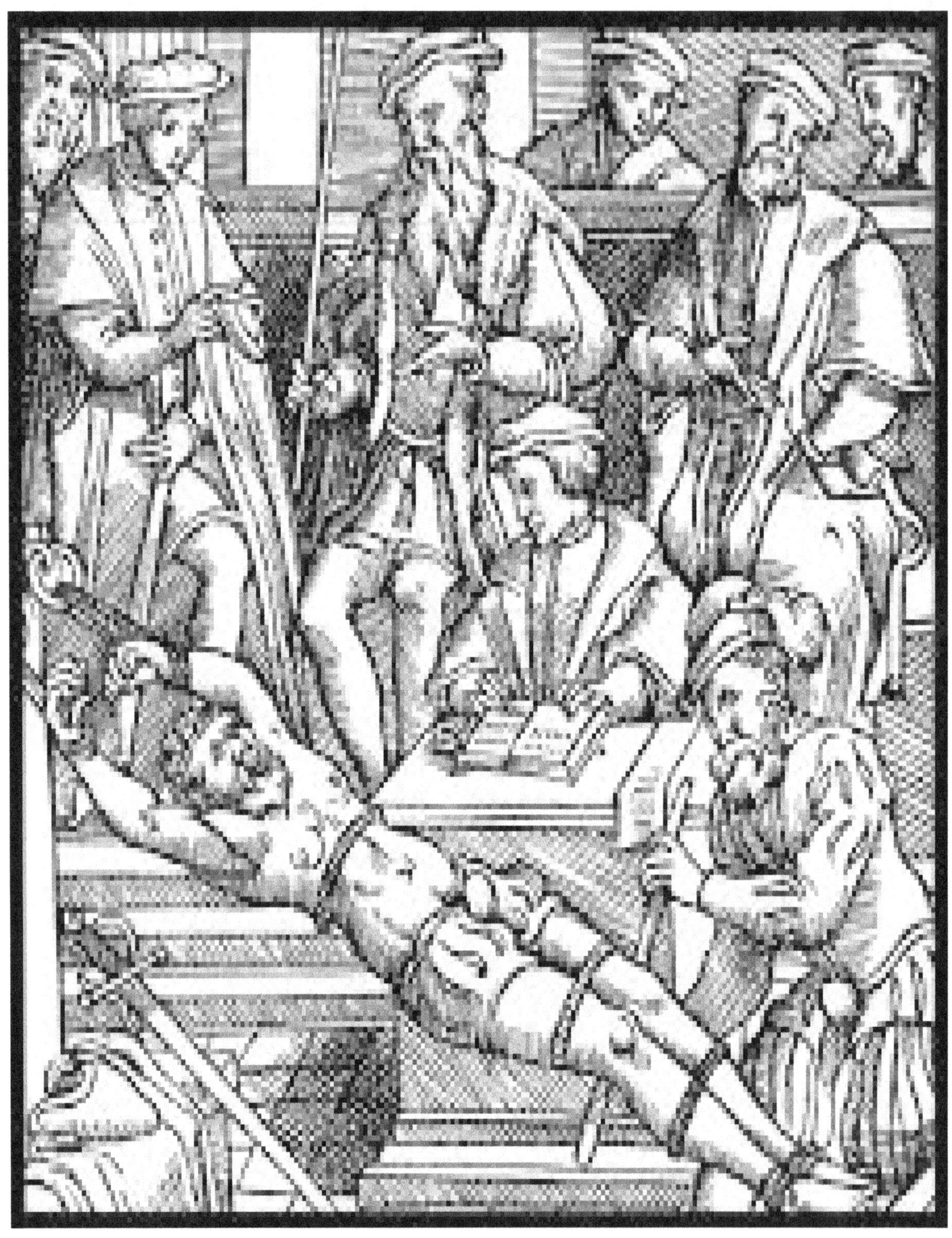

HISPANISSCHE INQVISITION

A royal beheading.

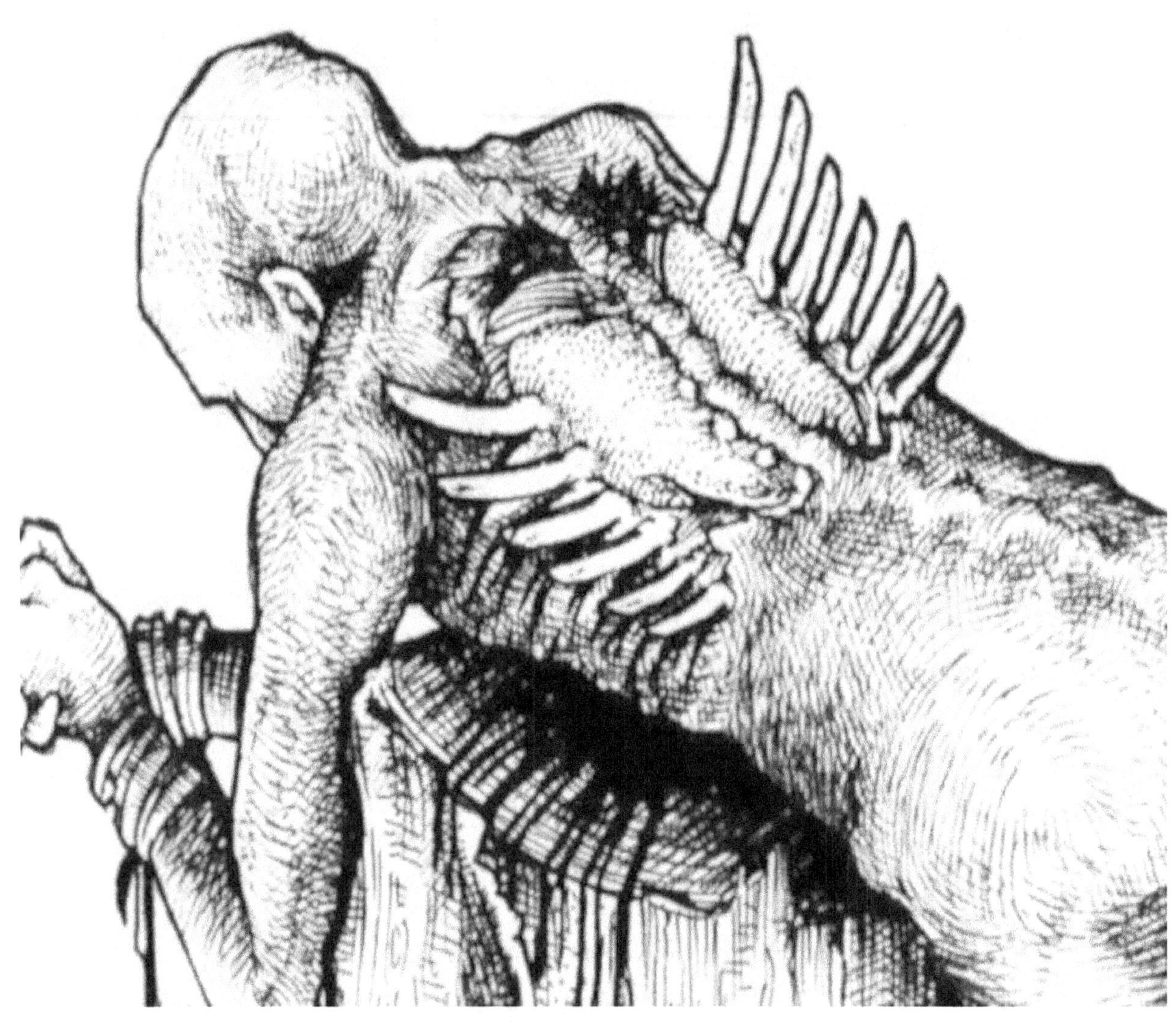

The horrendous "Blood Eagle."

ILLUSTRATIONS OF DEATH AND SATAN DURING MEDIEVAL TIMES.

197

M + S

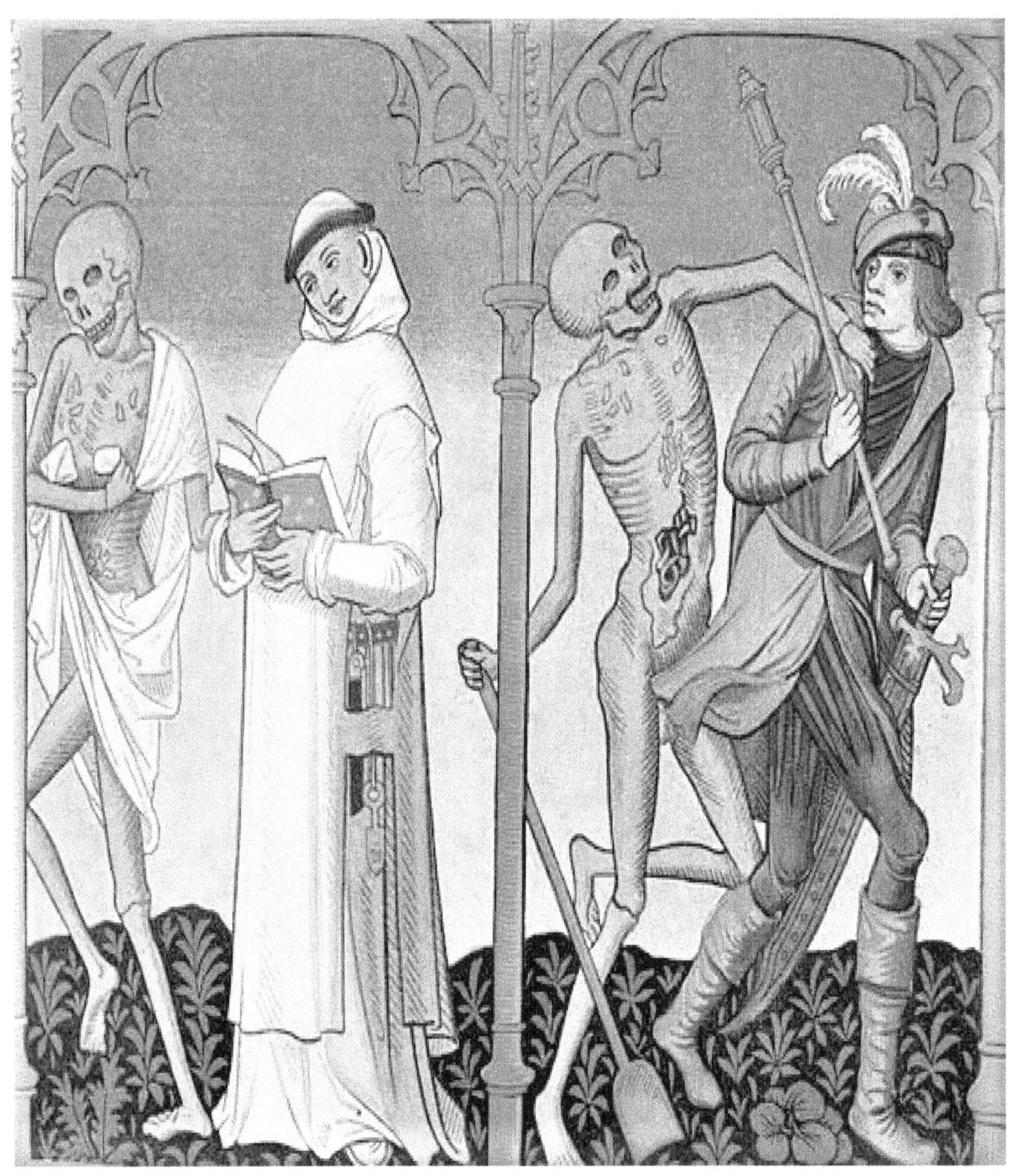

Medieval witch illustration.

I CLOSE THIS BOOK ON THE LIGHTER SIDE WITH THE INTERESTING U.S. PATENTED ITEMS.

OR, AS MOST WILL SAY, WTF?

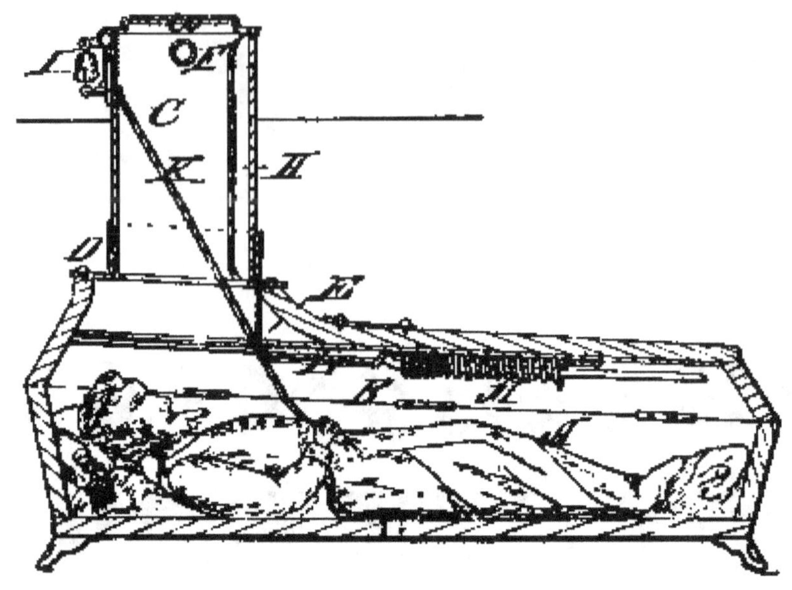

The Coffin Alarm. In case you Are buried alive. The body has a rope attached to a surface bell. Ring it, and hopefully, they will dig you up.

A Six Shooter for burrowing critters.

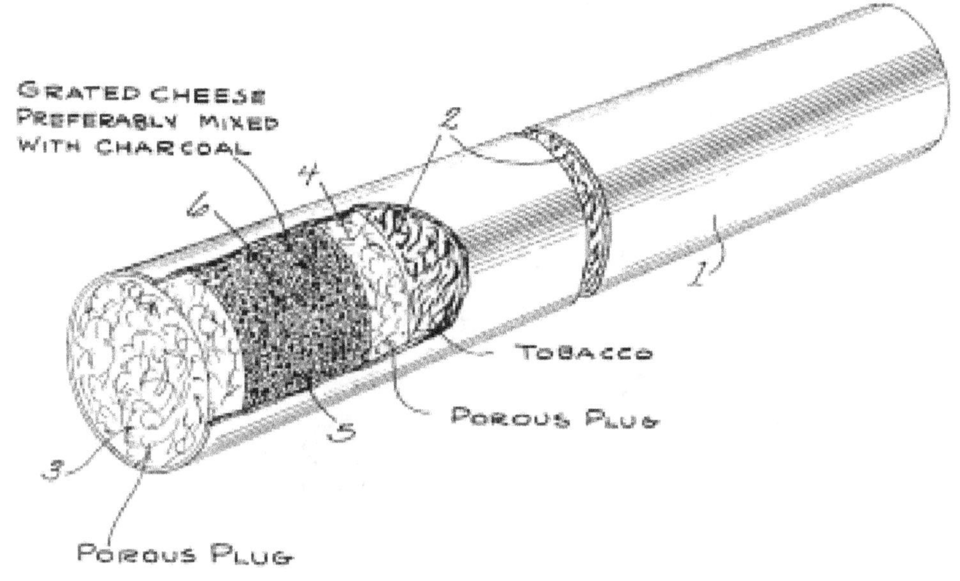

For Yummy Smoking, a cheese and charcoal Filter.

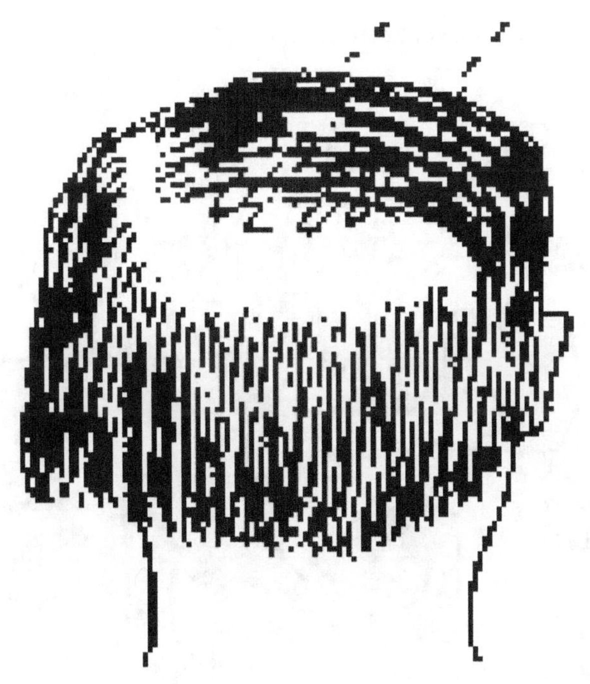

A U.S. Patent was issued for the comb over.

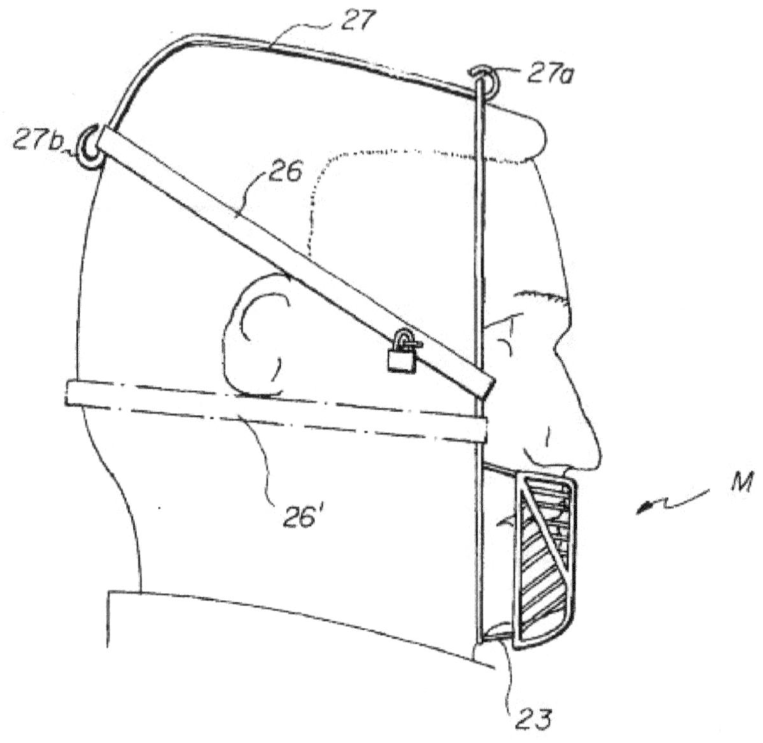

A locking mouth cover to stop overeating. Also, ideal for politicians to keep their mouth shut.

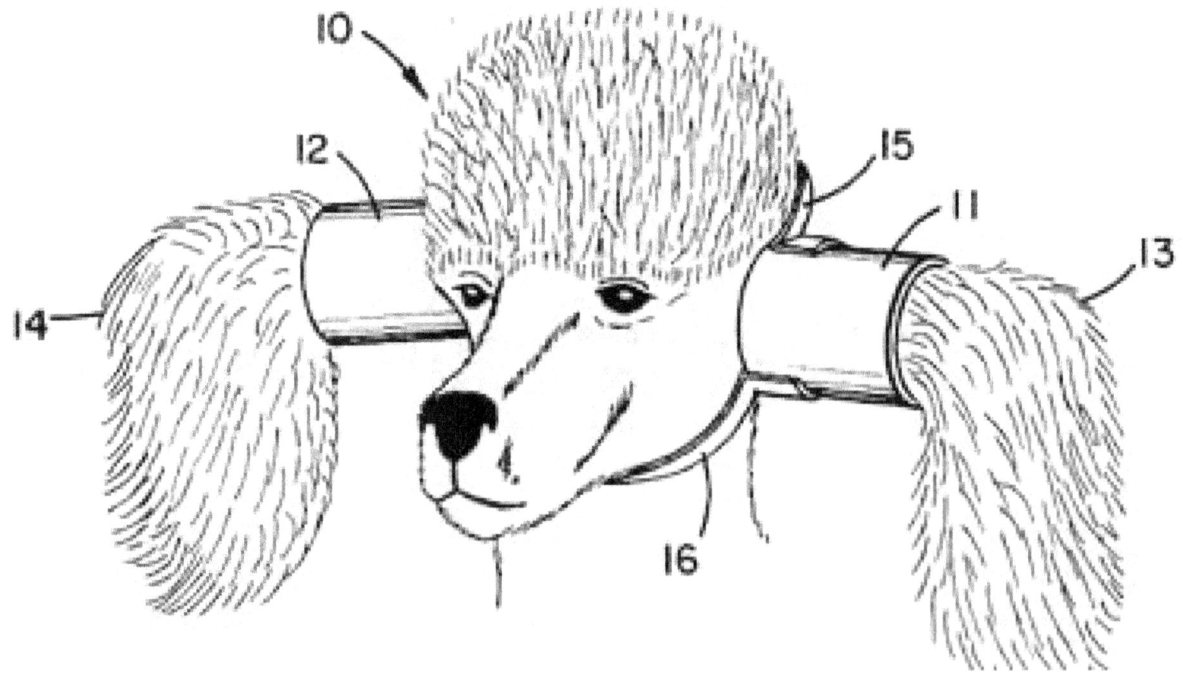

Ear covers to keep the doggies ears out of its food bowl when eating.

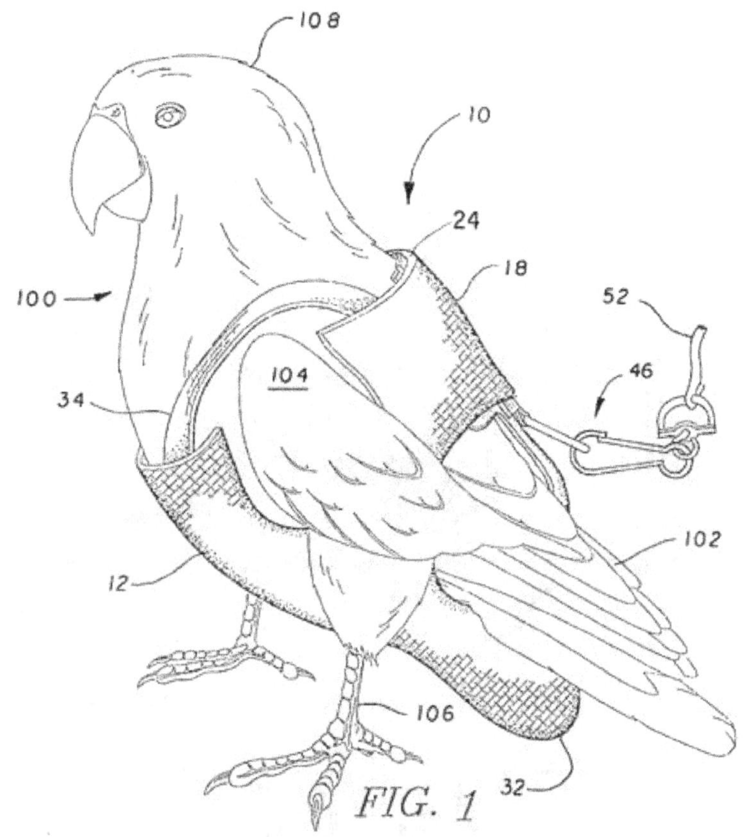

A diaper for birds.

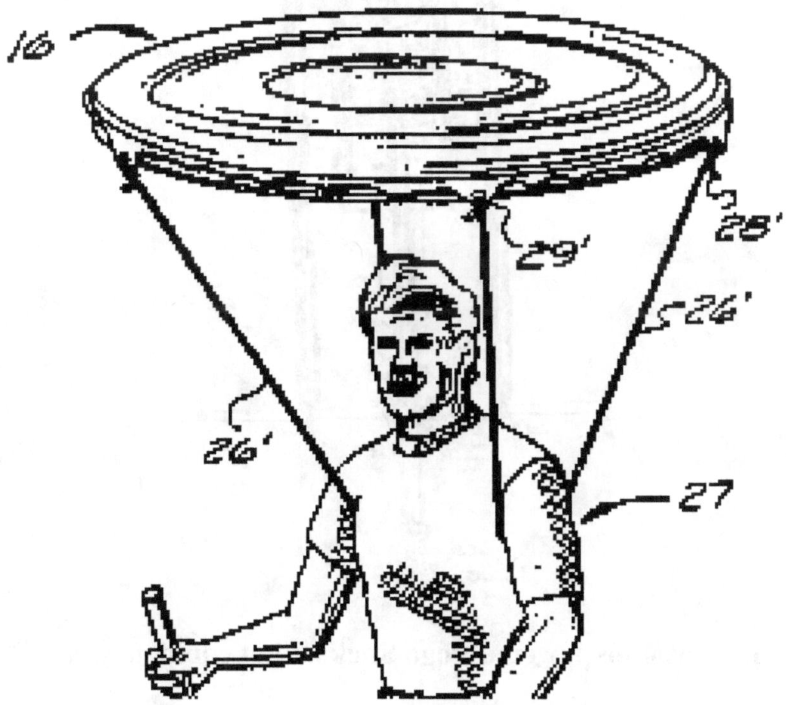

A helium filled sunshade. Great for standing under birds without a diaper.

213

An alarm clock that drops objects onto the sleepers head.

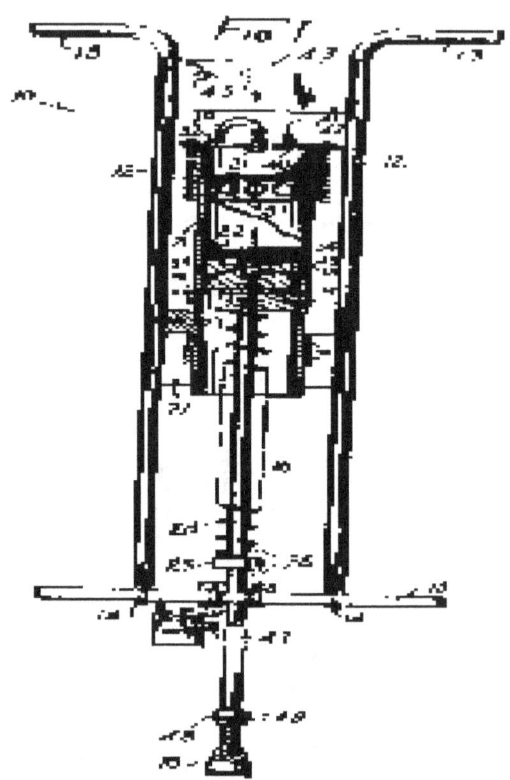

The gasoline-powered Pogo Stick. What could go wrong?

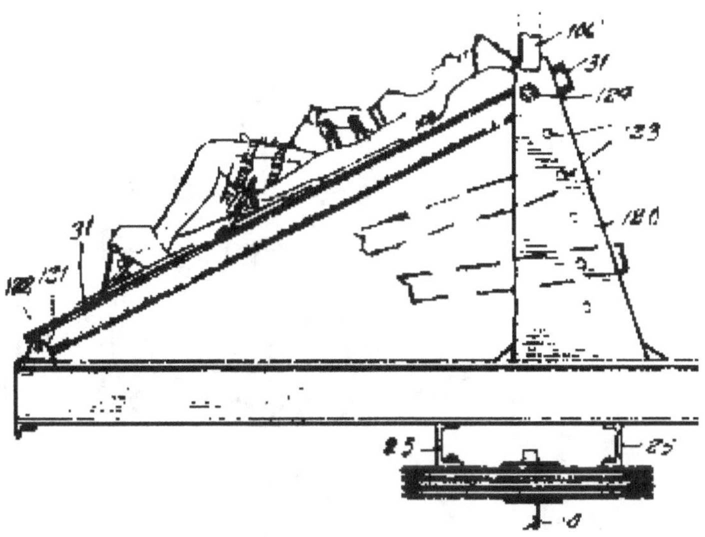

The centrifugal birth table. Spun at high speed, and the baby pops out.

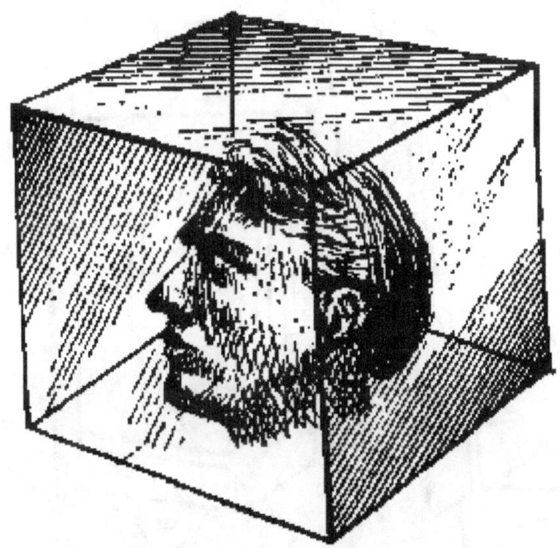

Keep your dead family members' head in a glass cube. It will always look as good as when they were living. The perfect gift.

A forehead rest for men when urinating.

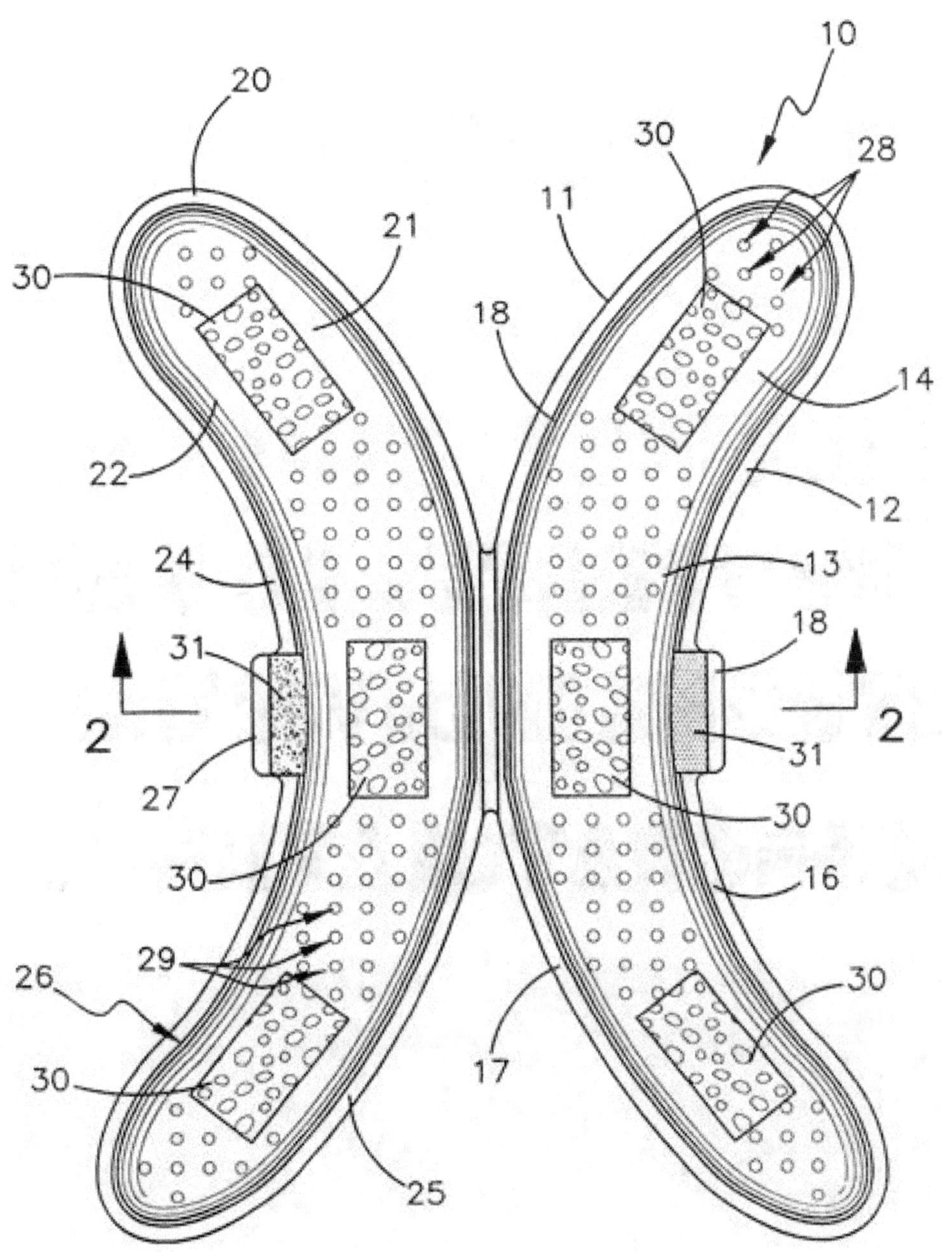

The always popular banana suitcase!

THE END.

MAKING IT THIS FAR DEMONSTRATES YOU ARE A STRONG INDIVIDUAL. CONGRATULATIONS.